C

A self-help guide to managing your career

(incorporating how to do it with Action Learning)

# CAREER WARRIOR

A self-help guide to managing your career

(incorporating how to do it with Action Learning)

**ROB STICKLAND**

Career Warriors engage in a lifelong quest to achieve their true potential driven by awareness of their true self-identity.

Watersmeet Tyne

I'm a proud supporter of Help for Heroes and would encourage readers to visit www.helpforheroes.org.uk to learn more about the work they do with wounded, injured, and sick servicemen and women.

© Rob Stickland, 2013

Published by   Watersmeet Tyne
                    2 Bishops Hill
                      Acomb
                      Hexham
                      Northumberland
                      NE46 4NH
                      England

All rights reserved. No part of this book may be reproduced, adapted, stored in a retrieval system or transmitted by any means, electronic, mechanical, photocopying, or otherwise without the prior written permission of the author.

The rights of Rob Stickland to be identified as the author of this work have been asserted in accordance with the Copyright, Designs and Patents Act 1988.

A CIP catalogue record for this book is available from the British Library.

ISBN 978-0-9576633-0-5

Book and Cover design by Clare Brayshaw
Cover Image © Ximagination | Dreamstime.com

Prepared and printed by:

York Publishing Services Ltd
64 Hallfield Road
Layerthorpe
York YO31 7ZQ

Tel: 01904 431213

Website: www.yps-publishing.co.uk

*For James and David ...*

*... Tall oaks from little acorns grow*

## CONTENTS

| | | |
|---|---|---|
| Acknowledgements | | ix |
| Permissions | | xii |
| **PART 1** | **Becoming A Career Warrior**<br>Setting the scene, creating the imagery, rallying support | 1 |
| Chapter 1 | Do you want a career? | 3 |
| Chapter 2 | Advent of the Career Warrior | 13 |
| Chapter 3 | Meeting the career demands of a changing world | 24 |
| **PART 2** | **The Armour – The Weapons – The Wiles**<br>Taking the imagery into career, organization, and life | 33 |
| Chapter 4 | The Career Warrior's armour | 35 |
| Chapter 5 | Weapons for a Career Warrior | 45 |
| Chapter 6 | The warrior's wiles | 48 |
| **PART 3** | **The Journey And The Quest**<br>Finding the way and following the pioneers | 59 |
| Chapter 7 | Action Learning – and how to make it work | 61 |
| Chapter 8 | Keeping a learning journal – career as a story | 80 |
| Chapter 9 | Setting learning objectives | 87 |
| Chapter 10 | Learning from example – what Career Warriors say | 95 |

| | | |
|---|---|---:|
| **PART 4** | **The Treasure Chest** | |
| | A box full of career and life management skills | 101 |
| | Getting professional career guidance | 103 |
| | The MAP exercise: getting at your motivation, ability, and personality | 108 |
| | The Career Warrior's weapons: skills for career self-management | 113 |
| | Checking the quality of match: you – your job – the job you want | 142 |
| | *Super Trouper:* spotlight on Action Learning | 146 |
| | Examples of career objectives | 152 |
| | A framework for organizational good practice in career self-management | 157 |
| Notes to chapters | | 162 |
| Index | | 169 |

## ACKNOWLEDGEMENTS

I'm grateful to many people who have helped me by taking an interest in my work, by challenging my assertions, by drawing attention to weaknesses and recommending lines of inquiry, and by their encouragement.

In my earliest stage of mature academic development, seven years of part-time undergraduate study with the Open University enabled me to discover both untapped potential within myself and the attraction of psychology as a future career. As a direct result of this learning I abandoned engineering as a career and decided to retrain as a psychologist. I'm pleased to credit the Open University with changing the course and the quality of my life.

As a novice psychologist many people inspired me through their personal example and their passion for the profession. Peter Herriot, Head of Occupational Psychology at Birkbeck, University of London, where I completed the MSc in Occupational Psychology, nurtured my learning at a time of career transition for me. I was indeed fortunate at that critical stage of my career to study under such a distinguished academic, and one who was highly proactive in applying his research to the real world of work.

Leaving behind many years of military life to enter the world of psychology as a mature trainee was challenging, but hugely stimulating and exciting. This new chapter of my life began in a London based career guidance organization where I rapidly acquired the tools and techniques of practical psychology to the point of becoming qualified to work independently. My director, Joshua Fox, helped me greatly in this through his demanding but supportive tutelage.

Good fortune continued in the first years of my work as an independent psychologist when John Arnold, Loughborough University Business School, accepted me as a member of his career seminar series funded by the Economic and Social Research Council. In that two-year programme I experienced what was for a non academic a rare opportunity to absorb the knowledge and experience of thirty academics, managers, and consultants deeply steeped in the field of career theory and practice. John continued to be a helpful network contact, sharing his own ideas as well as helping me through discussion and debate on my work.

During my PhD programme at the Revans Institute for Action Learning and Research at the University of Salford, David Botham, Institute Director and my research supervisor, was both an inspiring teacher and a source of steadying support, ever ready to challenge but in the most gentle and unobtrusive way so that often you didn't know you'd been challenged until you went away and thought about it. I have particular cause to be thankful to David for his comfort and encouragement at a time of deep personal distress that temporarily de-energized my research commitment and direction. Also at the Revans Institute John Morris was a source of wise counsel at various stages of my project work, usually during seminars where he never failed to illuminate core learning issues but also during my induction process in recognizing and encouraging my vision. Bryan Allison was hugely helpful as my Action Learning set adviser in steering me through three years of concentrated Action Learning. And in the final stages of my thesis Bryan Allison, John Morris, and Mike Pedler devoted time to reading and commenting on my work, giving me a wealth of feedback of inestimable value for which I'm truly grateful.

Like many others I owe a great deal of my learning to the late professor Reg Revans, internationally acknowledged as the father of Action Learning. Without his influence there would be no Revans Institute where I was privileged to undertake my PhD research (now the Revans Academy for Action Learning and Research at the University of Manchester Business School). On a more personal note Reg kindly and gently helped me to a new way of looking at myself in the context of the world.

In working through the research programme on which this book is partly based I acknowledge the unstinting help of Greater Peterborough Chamber of Commerce, Training, and Enterprise. In particular it was through the support and enthusiasm of Roy Brown, Deputy Director of Business Link and committed champion of learning, that I was able to gain access to the pool of people essential to my fieldwork. For that I'm hugely grateful to Roy.

I owe a special debt of gratitude to all the people who participated as respondents in my research project, especially to those who accepted the challenge of becoming a Career Warrior. I earnestly believe their participation will contribute to a means of bringing career self-management within reach of many others and I hope they will find opportunities to pass on their knowledge and experience.

Throughout the book I use a number of examples taken from my case notes over the past twenty-five years. Where it's been possible to trace these individuals I've obtained their permission to use extracts from their notes and agreed with each of them whether I should use their real name or invent one. To protect the anonymity of the people I've not been able to trace I've used pseudonyms and avoided any identifying reference to their employer or location. I feel privileged to have been allowed to share the life and career experiences of these and the many other people I've coached, and I thank them all warmly.

Finally I gratefully acknowledge the role of my wife, Wyn, in creating the space that has allowed me to follow a vision through many years of part-time study and research. Those who have been there before me will understand the nature and meaning of this tribute.

# PERMISSIONS

I gratefully acknowledge the individuals and organizations listed below for granting me permission to use material for which they hold copyright. In each case copyright resides with those individuals and organizations.

Contact details for the National Careers Service UK and Northern Ireland. The Skills Funding Agency, Cheylesmore House, Quinton Road, Coventry, CV1 2WT, and the National Careers Service.

Contact details for Careers Wales. Career Choices Dewis Gyrfa, Ty Glyn, Unit 1 Brecon Court, William Brown Close, Llantarnam Park, Cwmbran, Torfaen, NP44 3AB.

Contact details for Skills Development Scotland. Skills Development Scotland, Alhambra House, 45 Waterloo Street, Glasgow, G2 6HS.

© The Action Test, The Learning Test, The Real Problem Test (Part 4, *Super Trouper*). Professor Mike Pedler, Henley Business School, University of Reading, UK.

© The Learning Triangle illustration (Chapter 8, and Part 4, *Super Trouper*). Dr Donna Vick, Director, Revans Center Global, USA (donna.vick@revanscenter.com).

© Photograph of Sycamore Gap, Roman Wall, Northumberland, UK (Part 4, Stress Busting visual). Andrew Stickland (andrewstickland@googlemail.com).

*Search for the Hero*
Words and Music by Paul Heard and Michael Pickering
© 1995 EMI MUSIC PUBLISHING LTD. and UNIVERSAL MUSIC PUBLISHING MGB LTD. All Rights for EMI MUSIC PUBLISHING LTD. Controlled and Administered by EMI BLACKWOOD MUSIC INC.
All Rights for UNIVERSAL MUSIC PUBLISHING MGB LTD. in the U.S. and Canada Controlled and Administered by UNIVERSAL MUSIC MGB SONGS
All Rights Reserved International Copyright Secured Used by Permission
*Reprinted with Permission of Hal Leonard Corporation.*

*Search for the hero* words and music by Mike Pickering & Paul Heard © Copyright 1994 Universdal Music Publishing MGB Limited. All Rights Reserved. International copyright secured. Used by permission of Music Sales Limited.

"Search For The Hero" Words and Music by Paul Heard and Mike Pickering © 1994, Reproduced by permission of EMI Music Publishing Limited, London W8 5SW.

# PART 1

## Becoming A Career Warrior

Setting the scene, creating the imagery, rallying support

# CHAPTER 1

> *Life can only be understood backwards;*
> *but it must be lived forwards.*
>
> Søren Kierkegaard, Danish philosopher, 1813-1855.

## DO YOU WANT A CAREER?

### THINK ABOUT IT

Strange question to ask at the beginning of this book? Not at all! Not everyone finds their satisfaction in life through their career. For some a job is a job, a way of earning enough money to be able to get on and do whatever feels important in life. Home and family, sport, travel, cars, socializing, whatever. So let's get that question out of the way first. There's absolutely nothing wrong with not wanting a career and many people live perfectly happy and satisfying lives without one. So if this is you be happy and be satisfied – unless I can persuade you that living a career that's right for you can be immensely rewarding and fulfilling and help bring you even more happiness and satisfaction in your life. Read on then, and even if you aren't persuaded I'm sure you'll find something of use to you.

### FOR THOSE THAT DO

For many people there's a desire to have more from work than just a wage. In my experience as a career coach, having taken thousands of people through career analysis and guidance, what people tell me they want, and what is so often missing from their lives, is job satisfaction and a sense of fulfilment in their life through work. Of course money, status, promotion are also important because we all need to maintain a reasonable quality of life for ourselves and our families. But many people yearn for a higher level of attainment that brings satisfying and life fulfilling work. If you recognize that then let this book be the key that opens up such an opportunity for you.

Listen to Janet, a shop assistant, writing about how she found job satisfaction.

> 'Once I had been to see you I could clearly see I was in the wrong profession and should be in a more caring job. I immediately applied to a London hospital and was accepted onto their course for dental nurses. After becoming Student Dental Nurse of the year I remained at the hospital and am now working on the consultants' clinic in oral and maxilla facial treatment. I have been most happy in myself and have not looked back since.'

Being in the job that's right for you is satisfying because you are working at something which matches your motivation, for which you have the right ability, and to which your personality is well suited. And do take the hint from Janet – when you get it right, not only do you feel good about yourself, you succeed at what you do.

The sad thing is so many people don't truly feel in tune with their work. And whilst they can list what it is they don't like about it they find it very hard to describe what it is they want. The problem is we don't have an easy way of translating those inner feelings into the language of career. So we feel stuck, and that causes irritation and a sense of frustration at not being able to move forward.

This book is written for all those people who feel stuck in their career thinking and don't know how or where to begin. Work through the chapters and you'll develop the knowledge and skills to understand the career management process. Then take responsibility for the management of your own career and find the satisfaction and success that comes with reaching out for your true potential.

## BUT WHY SHOULD I DO IT FOR MYSELF?

You may not be in employment, or you may be working from home, or doing voluntary work, or part of a small firm with no training and development staff, or at home looking after the children - so you're on your own without a personnel department to turn to. If you're part of a larger organization you may well ask, 'Shouldn't my manager and my organization be looking after my career?' Well of course they should! Some do, but many don't. What happens in most organizations is that a select few get the special treatment – the sponsored courses, time off for education, management development programmes, development centres, and so on. But for most it's a very limited amount of training and development, and then usually aimed only at what the organization needs rather than what you need or want.

So there's one good reason. If you don't look after your own career who will? Here's another: who knows you better than you? So why trust anybody else to get it right for you? And for those in employment here are three more reasons for managing your own career:

### Shrinking Workforce

There surely can't be anybody who hasn't noticed organizations are doing more and more with fewer and fewer people – sadly a necessary response to economic recession, new technology, worldwide competition, and ever growing customer power. Call it downsizing, rightsizing, delayering, becoming lean and mean. They all mean the same thing: more to do and fewer people and less time to do it.

The upshot is that whereas in the days of high employment it was possible to keep your head down and coast along, nowadays the spotlight is on everyone because everyone's performance is crucial in a smaller labour force. So it makes sense to manage your performance at work in a way that ensures you're wanted rather than redundant at the next restructuring.

### Short Termism

Because the future is much less predictable than it used to be it's harder for organizations to stick to long-term plans. They have to react quickly to market changes to survive. So your career is seen in terms of developing you to meet the current needs of the organization. But you need to see your career as a long-term, maybe a lifetime, issue. This will not be at the top of your employer's agenda. So here you are, on your own again.

## *Career Transitions*

Shrinking workforce and short termism mean people may need to change career track five, six, or seven times over their working lifetime these days. You need to manage those changes. Nobody can reasonably expect their employer to do that for them.

### AN ASTROLOGER IN WAITING

*Martine, a graduate in French and Russian, sought career analysis when she was feeling depressed and frustrated by her work as a financial services business manager. Her work required heavy commercial focus when what she really wanted was closer involvement in helping people. Clearly out of tune with her work role, and the business focus of her departmental managers, this scenario led Martine to anxiety and weakened self-confidence.*

*It wasn't difficult to pinpoint the source of Martine's frustration. With exceptionally strong aptitude for communication and a deep desire to respect and value people as individuals, Martine needed to take a lead role in helping people achieve their potential. For her this needed to be a highly interactive activity where she could feel instrumental in the development of others. She needed to feel that what she was doing was worthwhile. Her warm, sensitive, and open nature were right for this kind of career role.*

*Armed with this knowledge, and knowing she couldn't be happy in her present career role, Martine took the risk of leaving her company without a job to go to. After a brief spell of part-time and temporary work Martine followed up a long-term interest in astrology with full-time study, and within two years achieved with distinction the Diploma in Astrology. Qualified now as a professional astrologer, Martine has launched her own business and is feeling very happy with her career move. Being in the right kind of career role has given her the self-confidence to face the future with strength and optimism.*

## SO WHY CAREER WARRIOR?

One thing my experience and my research has shown me is that most people are interested in their career and do want to do something about it for themselves. Some have no problem doing this, but for many the barriers are too big. How do I start? What are the steps? How do I keep track of things? Will I understand the language of careers? These are the kind of questions people ask, and the kind of problems that stop people going ahead and managing their own career.

Yes, career is complex. That's why we have highly trained and specialized career coaches. And yes, in an ideal world there would be enough support and help for everyone. But no, there isn't. So except for a very few enlightened organizations we sink or swim on our own.

It was my experience of these issues at first hand, initially in building my own career and later as a manager and as a career coach, that led me to look for a solution that would help people help themselves. The solution had to be simple and it had to have a structure people could understand and follow. Because I found people could understand things better when they built their own career story around simple mental images (ladders, road maps, brick walls are good examples), I settled on using mental imagery as the building block of a structure people could easily keep in their head. The image I've chosen is that of a Career Warrior. Here's how it looks:

Imagine yourself as a modern day warrior setting out on a lifelong quest in search of a satisfying and fulfilling life. Like warriors of old, you need armour, weapons, and wiles to protect and aid you on your journey. The Career Warrior's armour is self-knowledge, the weapons are a range of organizational skills, and wiles is about using your wits to navigate your career through uncertainty.

> **So how about you start your career quest right now? Begin the thinking process by dreaming up your own Career Warrior mental image – a bit like the avatar of computer gaming but carried inside your head instead of in cyberspace.**

I use the warrior image because my experience of working life is that the military metaphor is widespread in the structures, the behaviour, and the language of organizations. Read the business pages of any newspaper and you'll see what I mean. To help you get it right, these ideas are expanded in Chapters 2 and 3, and developed in depth in Chapters 4, 5, and 6. Use these chapters to build on your image and you'll have the tools you need to follow your own personal career quest.

Most of the world's cultures have some warrior or heroic figure, so your choice of mental image is open to wide interpretation. It can be real, mythical, religious, warlike, ancient, or modern.

Some people (though not many) have told me they feel uncomfortable with an image of themselves as some kind of warrior. The answer is simple: understand the idea of Career Warrior then translate it into whatever kind of mental picture you feel is right for you. You could, for example, use the image of a pilgrim. The armour is a cloak, the weapons are essentials for the pilgrimage such as a staff and cooking pots, and the wiles remain the wiles since pilgrims too must often use their wits to survive. So you need be limited only by your own imagination.

## THE THINKING BEHIND THE BOOK

We're concerned here with the psychology behind career management. The aim is to help you understand yourself and how to translate that knowledge into career terms so that you can manage your own career. It's not about how to write a CV or how to prepare for interviews or how to move jobs. There are stacks of good books on those topics on the shelves of libraries and bookshops. But before you use them the essential first step is to know yourself. Without a good understanding of yourself you'll be feeling your way in the dark.

The book is designed as a self-help guide, but this doesn't mean you have to work alone. It will be important to use the skills you develop to enlist the help of people who can be of use to you in your career journey. A moment's thought will tell you it's much more beneficial to work with other people than to work entirely alone, if this is possible for you.

Taking this idea further, whilst you'll learn a lot about career self-management from simply reading the book and putting its ideas into practice, you can seriously increase the drive power behind your success by getting together with a few like-minded people in a process known as Action Learning. If you want to know more about Action Learning at this stage take a peek at Chapter 7 where the first few pages will give you sufficient insight to start thinking about it.

By working through the book you'll be taking responsibility for control of your own life and destiny, steering your career in the direction best suited to your talents and, if you can, seeking to work in conjunction with people of similar interests who will provide the challenge and support which will greatly increase the speed and effectiveness of your success.

Don't worry, though, if you aren't in employment or don't want a job. Use the book to shape your life. For job just substitute home maker, parent, retiree, volunteer, or whatever. It's being in control of your life that will bring you a sense of fulfilment with it.

Personally I see career and life as the same thing. Sad? Not for me! I just believe we should strive to fulfil our potential by following a path through life that makes best use of our gifts. I know you can do it too – if you really want to.

### THE LAWYER BEHIND BARS

*Geraldine described life as an independent private practice lawyer as 'like living behind bars'. Long days, taking work home, seven days a week working left no time for relaxation, fun, or relationships. After taking time out to work on her career Geraldine made a shift within her profession by joining the Crown Prosecution Service. Here's how she saw it on looking back.*

*'The advice given – to work within a large organization and find more intellectually stimulating work – was exactly right. I have found tremendous job satisfaction in the work I am now doing. Since my working environment is*

*more structured than when I worked for myself it also means I can take time off and do not have to work excessively long hours.'*

*In Geraldine's case her profession was right for her. It was just the work environment that was wrong.*

## THE STRUCTURE OF THE BOOK

The book is divided into four parts. Part 1 explains the meaning of Career Warrior, how the idea came about, and why it's important to acquire the knowledge and skills to take responsibility for the management of your career and your life. Chapters 1 and 2 set the scene for career self-management and introduce the idea of reducing the complexity of career theory to a simple structure based on the mental image of a Career Warrior. For those who are interested, and for those looking to influence managers or employers on the benefits for the organization of supporting career self-management, Chapter 3 gives the reasoning behind the idea of Career Warrior.

In Part 2 we uncover some highly practical career self-management skills, developed partly from research but largely through many years of working with people from all walks of life and all levels of ability. Chapter 4 takes you through the crucial first step of establishing self-awareness, including information on how to get professional help with your career thinking. The essential skills you'll need to acquire for successful career self-management are highlighted at Chapter 5, and Chapter 6 shows how to become skilled in navigating your career using a simple model.

Part 3 focuses on support mechanisms for making career self-management work effectively. Included is the process of Action Learning, a well tried and exceptionally powerful learning method which brings together like minded people for their common benefit. All the information needed to start up and manage a self-help group is in Chapter 7. But if you are going to work alone don't worry – all the information you need for that is in the remaining chapters of the book. The benefit of keeping a log or journal of your learning is emphasized in Chapter 8 together with details of how to go about it. In support of this, Chapter 9 explains the importance of setting career objectives and gives specific examples. Finally, in Chapter 10, there are a number of personal illustrations of how Career Warriors have benefited from the programme.

I call Part 4 the Treasure Chest because in it you'll find explanations and exercises which are jewels of information for career self-managers. These are the tools of my trade as a career coach which I've developed over many years of working with hundreds of people seeking career analysis and guidance. You'll be directed to the Treasure Chest from the various chapters as and when you need to work with the information there. And each part of the Treasure Chest is cross-referred back to the chapter that gives the background to the topic so you can dip in and out if that's your preferred method of learning.

I hope you'll also find inspiration from the career stories I've used throughout the book. All of these are true stories taken from my work.

## ABOUT MY MISSION

Søren Kierkegaard, in the quotation at the head of this chapter, reflects that life can be understood only by looking back. I agree it's easier to understand events in your life with the benefit of hindsight, but you can develop a good understanding of how your life could be lived by looking forward. And you can use this understanding to dramatically change the direction and purpose of your life.

The way to do this is to study the experience of those who've gone before you. With today's widespread and easy availability of books, libraries, and the internet it's not difficult to access that experience, to learn from it, and to introduce that learning into your own life so you can begin to visualize a different you and begin to understand how your life could be.

What I'm setting out to do here is to offer you my experience, and the experiences of the many people I've coached over the years, so you can use that learning to help yourself establish your own sense of life direction and purpose. The idea is not to become a clone of someone else but to use the thinking and structure of the book as a starting point in embarking on your own career quest. That way you shouldn't have to wait until you're old enough to look back and discover what might have been.

In writing this book I draw on my struggle to turn wasted school years into useful academic qualifications, my work as a leader and manager in the armed forces, and a career change into psychology that led me to specialize in career and management development.

My knowledge has been built on a mix of formal education, workplace learning, consultancy, and a vast number of one to one career coaching relationships. So this is a practical self-help guide, it's not an academic text. Chapter by chapter I take you through my thinking and development in the field of career coaching and introduce you to the processes I use to help people identify and achieve their potential.

In doing this it's often difficult to separate what I've learned from experience from what I've learned through education and research. In truth, each feeds the other to give some fresh insight. Where I've included direct copies of the work of others I've added the appropriate citation alongside the work. Otherwise, to avoid interrupting the flow of a self-learning text, I've included a notes section at the end of the book to acknowledge the major sources from which I've drawn inspiration.

**NEXT CHAPTER**
In the next chapter I tell the story of how I came up with the idea of Career Warrior and what it means for me. Read it if you:

Are interested in understanding the origins of Career Warrior.

Want more background to help you form your own mental image.

# CHAPTER 2

> *You've got to search for the hero inside yourself*
> *Search for the secrets you hide*
> *Search for the hero inside yourself*
> *Until you find the key to your life.*
>
> M People, Bizarre Fruit II, *Search for the Hero.*
> © (see permissions)

## ADVENT OF THE CAREER WARRIOR

### MUSINGS ON A TRAIN

I can pinpoint precisely the day the idea of Career Warrior first came to mind. The learning journal I keep to remind me of how and when I've picked up various thoughts and bits of knowledge tells me that Monday 13th November 1995 saw me on one of those cross-country rail journeys, returning home to Peterborough after visiting the University of Salford to discuss the idea of embarking on a five-year part-time PhD programme.

Travelling home my mind raced around the idea of turning forty years of personal and practitioner experience of career development into a research project. Staring out of the carriage window into the moving tapestry of the beautiful Peak District, looking back over those years, my mind ran through the obstacles and the milestones. I thought of the sense of career and life satisfaction that largely trial and error learning had brought me. It felt as though I'd been involved in some kind of personal quest.

Being something of a dreamer the idea of quest conjured up mental images of the heroes of history and mythology. And suddenly I saw it!

Career is a lifetime quest. And like the warrior of old I'd spent many years testing myself in life, striving to achieve some career holy grail I wasn't sure really existed but confident that if I continued the search and remained true to myself there would, at the end of my journey, be an enormous sense of fulfilment that made life's efforts worthwhile. I'd become a Career Warrior.

This picture was exciting because it led me to a whole new level of interpretation. My personal quest had spilled over into a mission to help others take advantage of my experience. Over the years I'd coached people as a line manager, designed leadership and management development programmes as a training manager, and given career analysis and guidance as a psychologist. But I'd never thought to give people the one thing they needed more than all the advice: a mental image that pulled together a lifetime of learning into a simple structure they could use for themselves. Indeed, I'd never consciously looked inside myself to question whether such a structure existed. It had been enough to see personal development as simply an outcome of experience.

The Career Warrior idea would serve well as a means of helping people acquire a mental picture of what career development is about in the broadest sense. They could then dream up their own idea of warriorship according to their beliefs, upbringing, and culture.

## IMAGINE BECOMING A CAREER WARRIOR

Warriors of old set themselves apart by seeking to make their mark on the world through personal striving. Observation and contemplation of themselves and the world about them brought wisdom. Trials of strength and combat brought status and fame to the most successful. In the modern world I could see the idea of a new kind of warrior – the Career Warrior, with each of us becoming expert in the science and art of career warfare on the organizational battlefield. But beyond mere survival lies the ultimate aim of the Career Warrior: constantly reaching out towards the goals of career and life fulfilment. Such a search requires lifelong commitment to becoming master of one's own destiny. And, like the traditional warrior, the Career Warrior cannot embark on such a quest without first being properly furnished with the appropriate armour, weapons, and wiles.

## *Forging The Armour*

For a warrior, armour is the essential protection. But unlike the leather, chain mail, and steel of old the Career Warrior's armour is self-knowledge, perhaps more commonly known as self-awareness in the language of career. Without a strong sense of this it will be difficult to establish a career direction likely to bring job satisfaction and a feeling of fulfilment in life.

There are three plates in the Career Warrior's armour: motivation, ability, personality. Each is important and all must be worn and linked together.

> Motivation is about interests and values – what seems important in the context of life, finding enjoyment and job satisfaction, a sense of pride in achievement.

> Ability is what can be done. Skills, knowledge, experience, previous achievement – the sort of stuff you put in your CV. But it's also about aptitude – what may yet be achieved given discovery of your true potential and the right kind of education, training, and personal development needed to work towards it.

> Personality is about the kind of person you are. How you fit in with people, organizations, and situations.

A full and proper understanding of personal characteristics under these three headings of motivation, ability, personality – MAP for short – is the crucial starting point on the road to self-awareness. It's your armour because when all else around is in confusion it gives a solid reference against which to judge whether your career is proceeding in a direction likely to bring about what you want from it. So it protects the Career Warrior from wrong thinking.

Getting to understand your MAP isn't easy. As many self-developers have discovered for themselves it may be acquired through experience, through careful reflection on the course of life, or through introspection. You can begin the process by working through Chapter 4 which will give you a better understanding of your MAP and introduce you to the MAP exercise.

Do note though that discovering your true potential is much more difficult and may need the assistance of a professional career coach. There's more about this in Chapter 4.

*EX MARINE*

*TARGETS MANAGEMENT CONSULTANCY*

*Brian felt washed up. As a resource analyst in a large financial services organization he spent most of his time staring into a computer screen. The memory of the challenging and varied life which had once been his as a Royal Marines commando seemed far away. Now he felt frustrated and bored by a job that didn't use his talents. It seemed like he had nothing much to do and certainly had no sense of direction in his life. Worse, nobody in his organization seemed to care.*

*Career analysis highlighted very strong entrepreneurial motivation and a need to generate the flow of ideas. Brian's best aptitude was for work of a highly practical, hands-on nature, bringing expertise to bear on problem areas where he could use his excellent managerial potential. In personality he was highly independent with a willingness to explore new ideas, and he had the self-confidence to take the lead in things.*

*Energized by this analysis Brian threw off the lethargy in which his present job had enveloped him and took back control of his life. Within weeks he moved to a Further Education College as Conference Centre and Training Projects Manager. In parallel with his new job he studied for and gained the Postgraduate Certificate in Applied Emotional Intelligence and the Diploma in Performance Coaching.*

*A little over three years on from his unhappy days as an analyst Brian became a self-employed management consultant committed to the development of others. Back then he said, 'I knew I could make a difference but nobody would listen.' Now in the final stages of an MA degree in Professional Training and Development, Brian has built his own particular brand of organizational and personal development through strong emphasis on facilitation. 'I'm energized, dynamic, happy,' he says. 'The world is full of opportunities and I'm constantly striving to take them on board.'*

## *Acquiring The Weapons*

Armour alone, whilst a useful survival aid, is not sufficient for a campaign that will take you through periods of career uncertainty and confusion. For this the right weapons are needed. Not the spear, bow, and sword of the traditional warrior but a range of organizational skills from which you can select what is relevant and appropriate to particular circumstances.

There'll be little benefit in trying to acquire and memorize all these skills at once. Use them selectively when you find you need them to manage issues and problems as you meet them. That way you'll learn in the most effective and enduring way – learning by doing – or experiential learning to use the formal name.

The core weapons you'll need in your organizational skills armoury are discussed in Chapter 5 and supported in more detail by reference to the Treasure Chest, but listed here with brief notes to start you thinking about them.

### **Self-Marketing**

The ability and the confidence to sell yourself, not in an overbearing and pompous way, but appropriately and based on the insight of self-awareness. Acquiring good communication skills and keeping an up to date CV are important components here.

### Networking

Making and maintaining contact with people who can help overcome problems through the sharing of information and ideas. An excellent means of support when the going gets tough.

### Organizational Politics

Many people recoil at the thought of getting involved in organizational politics and go out of their way to avoid it. But do at least try to understand it since others will certainly use it. If you aspire to the highest levels of your organization it's unlikely you'll get there without some involvement in politics. But if it becomes impossible to handle don't waste time and energy cursing those who are political. Instead, reassess the direction of your quest and choose a different route. On the other hand, if you're willing to acquire the skill of politics, and use it wisely, you'll find it immensely helpful in accessing organizational intelligence and securing career support. But used without honour it's likely to bounce back and bring you nothing but distress.

### Interpersonal Skills

The skill and the art of respecting and valuing people, of listening to others, of being approachable.

### Proactivity

Not waiting for things to happen. Looking constantly for opportunities then figuring out how to exploit them. Delivering solutions rather than problems.

## Creating Opportunities

Developing awareness of opportunities within your organization, your profession, and the wider world that match your self-identity and your long-term career and life direction. This will involve acquiring the art of translating your personal characteristics of motivation, ability, and personality into career terms and an awareness of how to find information on appropriate career roles and the qualifications and experience necessary to achieve them.

## Leadership

Whether leadership of self or leadership of others, this is a valuable skill which often wins the day when other means have failed. It's not necessary to be a formally appointed leader to acquire and use leadership skills. Ownership of this weapon will give you a significant advantage in furthering your quest.

## Stress Management

The art of retaining a sense of control over the direction and quality of your life. Understanding how to maintain a proper balance between physical and emotional wellbeing. This is not an optional weapon. It's essential for coping with the uncertainty and ambiguity encountered in present day organizational life.

## Action Learning

A form of networking where people meet on a regular basis to provide a forum in which they enhance their self-knowledge and solve problems that are preventing them from moving forward.

*Things were not going well for Suzanne. Her job as a computer programmer was taking her nowhere, and despite repeated requests for more demanding work her company offered her no help. She felt demoralized and unfulfilled, and because she felt so badly about her work she began to feel bad about herself. Soon the stress of unsatisfying work led to days off with sickness. The vicious spiral of bad work bad health, more bad work more bad health, kicked in.*

*It was at this time Suzanne took professional career guidance. Her real potential lay in science and technology based research and development, searching for creative solutions of practical benefit to people and society. She needed to do this in a highly active environment with lots of variety and frequent interaction with people. But in her present role, tied all day to a computer screen massaging other people's work, Suzanne's true potential lay undiscovered.*

*Feeling more confident from this self-knowledge Suzanne left her company and decided to build on her psychology degree by taking a full-time MSc in Ergonomics prior to a career change into that field of work. Ergonomics felt right, and a distinction in her dissertation reinforced this feeling. Now Suzanne is a senior human factors engineer with a global technology group. She presents at conferences and is sought after for her expert advice.'Life is just brilliant,' she says. 'I love my job, I'm much more relaxed and outgoing, and I do feel I am in a career where I can do well and make a difference. Life is much happier now.'*

## *Discovering The Wiles*

Every warrior develops a certain air of cunning, an artfulness that aids battle through mental alertness to opportunities which might be exploited by wits rather than strength of arms. For the Career Warrior this lies primarily in the art and skill of career navigation – the ability to navigate a career through the organizational fog of uncertainty and constant change. The ability not to lose sight of longer-term goals when shorter-term issues confound the progress of the quest. And the wisdom to see that it's not always possible to reach the goal by moving forward on a predetermined path. That sometimes the flexibility of taking a detour can be a more prudent means of achieving an end.

So how does this work in practice?

Having put on the armour of self-awareness it's vital never to lose the sense of self this gives. Personal characteristics of motivation, ability, personality become a navigation instrument, a template against which the worth and value of each career move, each organizational initiative exploited, each development opportunity pursued is judged. The template will indicate which career opportunities are an appropriate match and which are inappropriate. It's then for you to judge whether inappropriate opportunities should be abandoned or whether they might provide a useful detour. But because you have a template against which to make such judgements you'll have an awareness of the order of mismatch. The risk to the quest can then properly be assessed.

You must, however, constantly reappraise the quality and strength of your armour through critical self-examination, through updated career thinking, and through debate with those you've learned to trust. Matching self to a career path isn't a static once-and-for-ever event. It's a dynamic process that requires lifelong attention. Career navigation is the crucial wile that helps keep the quest on course.

See Chapter 6 to learn more about career navigation.

## WE CAN ALL FIND A HERO INSIDE OUR SELF

Not long after I'd put these ideas together I spent some time with two amazing young people – a couple, full of energy and emotional strength. Matt had bought the CD quoted at the head of this chapter for Kate as a birthday present. As I listened to Kate playing her birthday gift, the track *Search for the Hero* suddenly pierced my consciousness. For me it was electric. The chorus lines fitted exactly with the Career Warrior mental image. Take another look at the lines in the quote.

If you want to find the key to your life you have to spend time and effort searching for the hero inside yourself – your true self-identity.

The secrets you hide are your undiscovered true potential. For many people their true self is hidden from them by the person they've become, based on the way they've interpreted various life experiences (often wrongly) and the way people have influenced their thinking (often wrongly).

In giving lectures and seminars on career self-management I began to play that inspiring chorus, using the Career Warrior image to emphasize at the end of each line how it related to the search for self-identity. With some audiences it even sparked spontaneous singing and arm waving.

So? Go buy the CD or download the track. Play it frequently. Listen carefully. Allow the words and music to enter your consciousness. Sing the chorus in the shower. Sing it while driving. Anything to fix it in your head and remind you of how to identify and become the hero inside yourself. Soon your Career Warrior thinking will become a habit that will inspire and motivate you.

### HR MANAGER CHANGES IMAGE

*Belinda felt submerged by months of work on an HR project that required long hours in front of a computer screen and a high level of attention to detail. Due to the nature of the project the contact she had with people tended to generate conflict, so Belinda felt no sense of fulfilment in her work.*

*In fact Belinda's motivation centred on a deep concern for people and the need to interact with them at the level of emotions and feelings. She wanted to help people with their problems in a caring and supportive way that led them to improve the quality of their life. Belinda showed good all round aptitude, but with particular potential for the development of communication skills. In personality she was lively, outgoing, warm, and trusting. She wanted to work in co-operation with people rather than to manage them.*

*After career analysis Belinda set about making changes in her life so she could work more in tune with her characteristics. Building on her HR qualifications and experience, Belinda studied for and was awarded the Certificate in Counselling, and her love of colour and design encouraged her to train as a professional image consultant to add to the qualification she already held in beauty therapy.*

*Moving on to work as an associate career coach with a leading career consultancy company, Belinda was able to feel deeply involved in helping people through difficult periods in their lives. Alongside that work Belinda set up and now runs her own training and development company, focusing on the idea of personal image as the key to achievement of potential for both businesses and individuals. Belinda speaks with enthusiasm: 'My work is great, I love it to pieces. People are so interesting. It's hard work but I feel I've arrived at where I ought to be.'*

## CHANGE IS THE WINDOW OF OPPORTUNITY

Many people see change and the chaos it usually brings as frightening and to be avoided, and with growing organizational pressure they frequently respond by working harder and longer rather than working more effectively. Career Warriors welcome change and chaos because they bring them many opportunities to apply their knowledge of self (their armour) and the skills package they've worked at acquiring (their weapons) to enable them to practise the art of career navigation (the wiles). These are the keys to finding more effective ways of working, and this learning is available to you in Part 2.

## NEXT CHAPTER

Chapter 3 offers argument to support the idea of Career Warrior. It will be useful to those who wish to persuade others of the benefits of career self-management, and interesting to those who like to ask the question 'Why?'

But if you don't need it don't read it. Skip to Part 2 and the practical skills required to search for the hero inside yourself.

# CHAPTER 3

> *He aha te mea nui,*
> *He tangata, He tangata, He tangata.*
>
> *What is the most important thing in life?*
> *It is people, people, people.*
>
> Maori proverb, Christchurch Cathedral, New Zealand.

## MEETING THE CAREER DEMANDS OF A CHANGING WORLD

This chapter will interest the curious reader who wants to know why career self-management is so important. It will also help you in persuading your manager and your employer to support you in your efforts to take personal responsibility for your own career management. How? By using the argument of this chapter to show that doing so is a means to greater productivity and profitability.

But if the thinking behind Career Warrior is of less interest to you than the practical tips on managing your own career you can safely abandon this chapter. You have everything you need in the rest of the book.

### WHY CAREER SELF-MANAGEMENT HAS BECOME AN ISSUE

Writing the foreword to a book on careers in 1938, Sir Malcolm Campbell (holder of world speed records on land and water) described career choice as the great decision made at the crossroads of life when youth begins to merge into manhood or womanhood. Seventy-five years on, and with the opportunities for adult education and development that exist today, we no longer need to think of career as a one off choice immediately after school or university. Now we're encouraged to think in terms of lifelong learning and the opportunities that brings for moving on to new organizations and new career paths. This kind of career movement requires long-range career management – unlikely to be provided by your present employer who needs to focus on the job you do for them – so it's a task that needs to be taken on by you.

The world of work has also changed greatly since the 1930s, particularly over the past three decades or so. In Chapter 1 I drew attention to global trading, new technology, world economic recession, and customer power as factors which have combined to generate fierce business competition. As companies struggle for survival in this highly competitive world they turn inevitably to cost reduction programmes to reduce overheads, and, since the costliest element is usually people, it's people that have to go.

This isn't just within the business world. Public sector and not-for-profit organizations are not immune since they have to weather the same economic storms, absorb the same effects of new technology, and try to serve the needs of an ever more demanding society. So it's not surprising they have to adopt the staff reduction initiatives they see being applied in the business world.

In this atmosphere organizations have to make tough judgements about who's worthy of promotion and who's stuck in a rut, who they keep and who they let go. This turbulent environment makes the competition to hang on to our job tougher, so it makes sense to prepare for it.

## *The Impact On You*

It's in this scenario we find career confusion. As we've moved from the idea of career as a lifetime choice in youth to thoughts of shorter bursts in different organizations, or different skill areas, responsibility for long-term career management has necessarily shifted from your organization to you. That's because only you can make sense of career direction over the whole of your lifetime – maybe spanning five or more job moves. Of course there have always been those who understand the need for self-help in their career management and take responsibility for it. And it's true some people have been fortunate in hanging on to their jobs long term. But many of us have either come to rely on the organization managing our career for us or been content to jog along safe in the belief that the job will always be there.

**_Have you made the attitude shift required to see your long-term career management as something you should do for yourself?_**

Pause for a moment and reflect on the fact that your job is only as secure as your period of notice. And, by the way, what is your period of notice? If you have the misfortune to be told your services are no longer required, how much time will you have to find another job?

Doesn't it make sense then to be prepared by taking on the long-term management of your own career now?

It's not just about surviving cutbacks, it's also about making yourself the kind of employee who is so valuable to the organization that you're unlikely to appear on a redundancy list. You might, for example, adjust to the idea of sideways rather than upward progression, acquire the skills of coping with constant change, come forward with ideas to help increase productivity and cut costs, identify your strengths and use them to develop yourself, gain a qualification related to your work. Should redundancy become inevitable your careful preparation will help you focus on getting another, hopefully better, job more in tune with your strengths.

But there's a greater benefit in career self-management. Are you uncertain about your present career role? Do you feel out of sorts there? Well why not work out what kind of career would give you more job satisfaction and a better quality of life? Then aim to get there.

Whether your need is to survive where you are, to work towards a better career role in your present organization, or to find yourself a completely new career, you need to:

Accept responsibility for your own career management.

Develop a strong sense of self-identity through improved self-awareness.

Follow a structured approach to your career journey.

Career Warrior is designed specifically to help you with the second and third of these needs. You have to manage the first for yourself.

## *The Impact On The Organization*

An organization's success in a highly competitive world depends on developing the skills and potential of every employee, not just the chosen fast-trackers. Big issues for employers revolve around their people. Which of their staff are most committed to the success of the organization? Who has the attitude and skills needed to cut costs and improve productivity, and who is a passenger? How can we hang on to the best employees? How can we know which is which?

Of course there are other important issues such as finance, research and development, sales and marketing. But, in organizations, as in life, the Maori proverb at the head of this chapter reminds us that behind all these roles are people, and if the people aren't right the work won't be right. The organization will struggle to be competitive. And maybe struggle to survive.

What you'll find, though, is that whilst organizations acknowledge people as their greatest asset very few provide the right kind of career development support to harness the best of that talent. In the UK this sentiment has been echoed for years by bodies such as the Confederation of British Industry (CBI), the Chartered Institute of Personnel and Development (CIPD), and the Trades Union Congress (TUC), all frequently sponsoring or using evidence from universities and research bodies.

For example, CIPD research has identified people management as a critical factor in improving business performance but confirmed it as one of the most neglected aspects of organizational management. So if organizations aren't doing enough to identify the right and the wrong people they risk weakening their competitive edge and losing out in the battle for survival.

This book is not the place for a review of personnel policy and practice. There are shelves upon shelves stuffed with books and research papers on how good people management produces good business and efficient organization. The point here is to help you see you are much better placed than your employer to manage your career, and to encourage you – in your own interests – to use career self-management skills to demonstrate your value to the organization. So if you are in a position to influence your manager or employer with these ideas, do it. Working together will bring benefits to both you and your organization.

## THE CASE FOR CAREER SELF-MANAGEMENT

Bringing all these ideas together, the thinking behind Career Warrior goes like this:

> From an individual point of view modern careers involve greater movement into and out of organizations and across different types of work. Supporting this is greater access to adult education, giving more opportunities for career advancement and career change. So for an enjoyable and successful career in this atmosphere of lifelong learning and change the individual is the person best placed to manage it.
>
> Looking at employers, most are not helping people with career self-management despite research showing links between good people management practice and improved business performance. Those organizations that do support career self-management generally restrict it to the current work role or to a limited number of specially selected people. Failing to tap

people's full potential is a failure to maximize productivity and profitability.

There is a clear need for a simple self-help guide so individuals can manage their own career. Career Warrior meets this need.

The case for career self-management follows two strands: one that benefits individuals and one that benefits organizations. It's important to keep this balance in focus so that management can see some organizationally beneficial outcome from its investment in people, and so that people can see some benefit to themselves from engaging in activity that leads to organizational gain.

But frequently organizations are reluctant to spend money on helping people develop their career skills beyond the immediate needs of their job in case they decide to go and work elsewhere. And very often individuals resist attempts to involve them in organizational development initiatives, either because they see nothing in it for them or because they've grown to dislike their organization and don't see why they should do anything to help somebody who doesn't help them. Both of these views are hugely limiting, and it's to avoid this situation that we should focus on meeting the needs of both parties.

For individuals the argument is simple: organizations don't help you manage your long-term career so you have to do it yourself. It's fair to say that some organizations do provide good career management support, but the majority do not. When career management support is provided it's usually linked to the organization's needs rather than to the long-term needs of the individual. This is understandable although short-sighted. It's understandable because the organization pays you to do the job they want you to do. It's short-sighted because it fails to tap the broader range of your potential. You will know which world you live in. But if the organization is wrong for you, however badly you feel about it, do use your work environment to focus on managing your own career future. Yes, your employer will benefit from that – but so will you. It's better to construct your own light at the end of the tunnel than to continue to sit in the dark.

For organizations the argument is more complex. Supporting employees in their career and personal development contributes to productivity and profitability. But organizations don't seem to see this link. If they did they wouldn't ignore it. Even when people use their self-knowledge to leave and find a new job this is useful to organizations as it makes no business sense to employ people who don't want to be there. And it frees up the space to recruit someone better fitted to that role. So your task, should you choose to follow it up, is to help the employer understand the link between people and the bottom line.

## FOLLOWING GOOD PRACTICE IN ORGANIZATIONAL CAREER PROGRAMMES

The message of both experience and research is that employee development makes good business sense, yet both highlight the gap between what should happen and what does happen. The point of this chapter is to draw attention to this difference. From that position the need for a practical means of helping people to do for themselves what organizations are failing to do for them becomes evident.

You may be in a position to use the knowledge you've gained from this chapter to persuade your employer to introduce a career development strategy, but before you do so think carefully about whether your organizational culture is right for it. People have to want to participate. Forcing them won't work. When people do engage voluntarily in career self-management they become highly proactive about their work and their self-development. If your organization fails to recognize and support their growth the disappointment of unmet expectations could lead to serious backlash. So be sure you've read your organizational culture correctly.

I do believe that eventually organizations will come to see the economic benefits of properly supporting all their staff in their career development, and particularly in encouraging career self-management. But how far ahead is this day? Ten years? Twenty years? Can you afford to wait around until it happens? This is why I've developed Career Warrior. It's a way of helping people who want to get moving, get moving, with or without the support of their organization.

If you can persuade your organization to believe in a Career Warrior programme you'll advance the cause of support for career self-management. And in doing so you'll not only help the people you work with begin to see how they can achieve their true potential, you'll be starting a movement that will bring your organization rewards they hardly imagine possible. Listen to this director telling us how his six-strong business team benefited from a Career Warrior programme.

> *'A year plus, meeting every three weeks, is a long time to remain fully committed to a course of action, but they did. Over this time I have witnessed a significant increase in the awareness and ability of every one of these individuals. Notwithstanding that these are people working in the area of individual and organizational development, I know that such advances would not have been made if normal line management techniques were to have been employed. In general, the confidence of all individuals has taken a great boost. Self-belief and self-reliance has increased significantly. There is a much higher level of both self and team understanding. This has resulted in lead roles within the team being allocated more effectively, and individual development plans being compiled on more rigorous and informed criteria.'*

And to see what Career Warriors themselves have had to say about their experience, turn to Chapter 10.

If you are successful in persuading your organization to start up and support a Career Warrior programme, or if you have the authority to do it yourself, you need a good practice guide as a framework for your programme. You'll find one in the Treasure Chest in Part 4.

**NEXT CHAPTER**

The next chapter introduces Part 2 which describes the practical skills and knowledge needed for effective career self-management.

All three chapters of Part 2 are essential reading for the would-be Career Warrior.

# PART 2

## The Armour – The Weapons – The Wiles

Taking the imagery into career, organization, and life

# CHAPTER 4

> *Would that God the gift would give us*
> *To see ourselves as others see us!*
> *It would from many a blunder free us.*
>
> Loosely translated from Robert Burns, 1759-1796.

# THE CAREER WARRIOR'S ARMOUR

## PROTECTION FOR LIFE'S JOURNEY

In Chapter 1 I introduced the idea of using the mental image of a warrior to help you fix on a simple structure for managing your own career in terms of armour, weapons, and wiles. I invited you to become a Career Warrior. And to get you thinking about this I outlined in Chapter 2 what I mean by the present day equivalents of armour, weapons, and wiles. In this and the next two chapters I want to expand on those meanings so you can begin to construct a Career Warrior mental model to suit yourself.

Let's start with armour. Why do I say self-awareness is your armour? Well, when we get into difficulties with our career – could be a bad appraisal for example, or maybe you just pierced your boredom threshold and feel you're getting nowhere fast – we have a tendency to see faults and weaknesses within ourselves as the problem. But my experience of working with people in this situation has shown me that more often than not the problem is a mismatch between self and the job or self and the situation. It's rarely a weakness within the individual that's suddenly appeared from nowhere.

Situations change, and so do people. What was right for you six months ago may not be right today for all kinds of reasons. But if you have a good sense of self-awareness it's not difficult to work out how and why you and your career have drifted out of tune. That's why self-awareness is so important. It's the armour that protects you from negative thinking about yourself, and it's the key to finding a way forward that is right for you.

Without that protection, self-doubt creeps in. And, if the out of tune feeling is prolonged, pretty soon it leads to loss of confidence and self-esteem as we turn blame inwards. I call this period of career confusion the Snowstorm Effect because it reminds me of the Christmas toy in the form of a small plastic dome containing a tiny winter scene. When you shake it snowflakes swirl around inside and obscure the scene, but when you hold it still the snow settles and you can see clearly.

A career in crisis can be like that: a head full of swirling doubts, questions, and blame. Just when we most need to be able to stand back calmly and reason things out we feel submerged by the snowstorm in our mind. We desperately need some clarity. Well, clarity will come from a structured way of looking at who we are and where we're going in our career and our life. More than ever the need now is for self-awareness.

### REDUNDANCY OPENED A WINDOW OF OPPORTUNITY

*For most people redundancy hits hard, and so it was for Mac. He enjoyed his work as an insurance refund investigator so it was a big shock when his job disappeared. Fortunately Mac's company offered him outplacement, or, as I prefer to call it, career transition support.*

*Mac's career analysis showed his motivation and aptitude both strongly centred on communicating. He very much wanted to be able to advise and guide people by using his knowledge and expertise to help them resolve problems. Conscientious, and with a well developed sense of duty, his temperament was serious and cautious. He believed in the value to society of sensible rules for living, and he found satisfaction in the investigative work of righting wrongs.*

*In fact Mac was very well suited to the job he had just lost and had no need of a career change. Using the outcome of career analysis to widen his horizons he negotiated an opportunity in Housing Management where a 'right place right time' break led to a position as a fraud investigator. Mac's experience and his suitability for this kind of work soon brought him promotion into a management role, a position he is consolidating through part-time study which has already brought him the Certificate in Counter Fraud Studies and will lead on to a BA degree in Public Sector Fraud.*

*Mac now has more senior and better paid work than he had at the time he lost his previous job. He showed that with the confidence that comes from good self-awareness redundancy can be turned into a success story.*

## A STRUCTURE FOR SELF-AWARENESS

So what is this crucial basic tool of self-awareness? Awareness of what? And how do we go about getting it? And why have a structure?

Self-awareness is knowing about the personal characteristics that form our unique identity – what makes us who we are, how we think, what we believe, how we behave, how other people see us. This unique, or self, identity is made up of countless life experiences from infancy to the present time, some conscious some unconscious, but every one contributing to our sense of self based on the way we learn from our actions and from the way people react to us. So the importance of self-awareness is in understanding the make-up of our self-identity and how it leads us to think, feel, and behave. We need this understanding to make sure we steer our career and life in the right direction, and to avoid the mistakes that can lead to career damage through lack of knowledge about how we impact on others.

Relevant to this point I've always liked the lines written by Robert Burns quoted at the beginning of this chapter (though weakened perhaps by my attempt to make his strong Scottish dialect an easier read for the non-Scots). In my work as a career coach I've found that one of the greatest failings in managers is the inability to see themselves as others see them. If we don't truly understand ourselves we can't begin to understand other people – and how best to communicate with them, to motivate them, and to lead them.

Self-identity is an exceedingly complex topic, but for our purposes of career management you need concentrate on only three sets of information about yourself: motivation, ability, personality. This will enable you to construct a simple model of your self-identity sufficient to begin building your Career Warrior image.

One of the things people tell me they like most about Career Warrior is its structure. People like structure because it helps them make sense of things and gives them a framework to work on. But because everybody is different and because everybody needs freedom to develop in their own way, we don't want the structure to be too rigid: you need to see the structure as a framework on which you can build your own mental model.

Referring to the illustration below, an easy way to remember the route to self-identity is to think of the initial letters of the three words motivation, ability, personality – MAP – and to recall them as forming a triangle. You could also think of them as the three pieces of your armour.

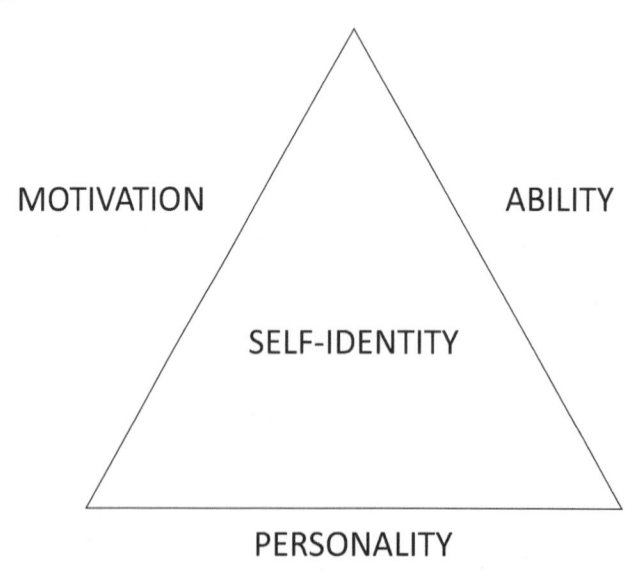

```
              /\
             /  \
            /    \
 MOTIVATION/      \ABILITY
          /        \
         /SELF-IDENTITY\
        /            \
       /_____\
          PERSONALITY
```

Why the triangle? Well it's important in managing your career to get all three in balance. You might have the right kind of ability to be successful in persuading and influencing but if you're quiet and shy, and not too keen on being pushy with people, it's probably not a great idea to go for a job in hard selling. A simple and obvious example, but getting your MAP out of balance can – and does – lead to a lot of career and life unhappiness. That's why self-awareness is so important, why I see it as the armour of the Career Warrior, and why your career journey needs to begin with it. So let's look at MAP more closely.

## *Motivation*

This is what gets you out of bed in the morning, the driving force in your life and your career. What it is about your life and your work that brings satisfaction, enjoyment, and a sense of pride in achievement. What you most want to spend time doing. Your interests and your values.

## *Ability*

What you can do. Your skills, knowledge, and experience gained from education, training, and on-job learning. But, as I highlighted in Chapter 2, there is a further aspect of ability and that is aptitude. Aptitude is the power we have within us to achieve more. The untapped potential that so often we feel is there but we find hard to pin down. I cannot recall ever working with a person who doesn't have some potential still to develop. Discovering it is not a simple task, and may require the help of a career coach, but it is so often the key to career satisfaction. Once identified and understood, the way to develop aptitude into ability is through education, training, and personal development.

## *Personality*

The kind of person you are. How you fit in with other people, with groups, with organizations. How you react to situations. How you feel about yourself.

*THE RADIOGRAPHER*

*Sheila worked in a global travel company as PA to a Human Resources Director. She was on top of her work, very successful in her role, and well thought of by her boss. Nevertheless Sheila felt there was more she could do with her life but lacked a firm sense of direction.*

*What motivated Sheila was methodical research and analysis where meticulous attention to detail was needed in solving problems that would benefit people. She enjoyed being with and working with people, but she preferred her work tasks to be involved with the management of information rather than the management of people. An aptitude profile showed Sheila to have versatility, but with particular potential for careers associated with science and technology. In personality she came across as reserved and self-reliant yet ever ready to put the needs of others before her own.*

*Exploring these new ideas reminded Sheila of a schooldays interest in chemistry and she decided to pursue this further by taking a part-time GCSE Chemistry course at the local college to add to the A levels she held in Psychology and Human Biology. An encouraging A grade success led on to a networking visit at the local hospital to test out ideas of a career in Radiography. Motivated by the visit, Sheila secured a full-time degree place at university and graduated three years later with an excellent upper second BSc in Diagnostic Radiography, including a first in her dissertation.*

*As a professional radiographer in a busy city hospital Sheila feels she is doing something really worthwhile. Already she is pushing to utilize her technological aptitude by broadening her role to include work with computerized and digitized equipment.*

## *A Question Of Balance*

People often confuse motivation and ability. Motivation is what we want to do, ability is what we can do. Some people love what they do best – others find that what they want to do is their area of weakest skill and aptitude. And sometimes, even when there's a good match between motivation and aptitude, the conditions under which you are working are wrong for your personality type. So for a happy and fulfilling career it's important to get all three aspects of your nature in balance. At the heart of achieving that balance is the process of career navigation, explained in detail in Chapter 6.

## **GETTING AT THE MAP OF SELF**

It's not difficult to see that identifying motivation, ability, and personality is at the heart of self-awareness. Doing it, though, is not so easy. People find it very hard to be truly objective about themselves. And when we ask friends and family to give us their opinion of us we often get to hear what they think we want to hear. So how do we get an unbiased picture of our personal characteristics of motivation, ability, and personality?

### *With Professional Career Guidance*

The best way is to use the services of a professional career coach. The coach will have training and qualifications in the specialist field of career guidance, and they'll have the experience to help you establish a proper sense of career direction. Finding the right person to help you is critical to your future. It needs to be taken seriously. That's why I've devoted a special section to show you how to go about finding professional guidance, the questions you should ask, and the safeguards you should look for. See the Treasure Chest in Part 4 to find this information.

Career coaches may use psychometric tests to help you identify your motivation, aptitude, and personality. Don't be put off by the language. Psycho simply means of the mind, metric means a system of measurement. Hence psychometric is to measure the mind. Of course in the sense we're talking about things, you can't really measure the mind. What the coach is looking at is your performance on paper and pencil or online tests of aptitude and your answers on motivational and personality questionnaires. Again, use the Treasure Chest to find the right questions to ask to know whether a person is qualified to use psychometric tests with you, and to heed the warning about the accuracy of psychometrics.

UK residents are entitled to a substantial amount of free help with their career development through government agencies (see the Treasure Chest). For those who want or need to go beyond this, for example to work with a psychologist who will help them with psychological testing and profiling, it will be necessary to pay for career advice. Sadly this often puts people off, even when they can afford it. My advice is to see career guidance as an investment rather than a cost. There's no better investment in your future than to sit with an expert adviser working together to form a good picture of your self-identity, pinpointing your strengths and your development needs, and shaping all this information into a plan to build on your potential. You'll find the developing process of self-awareness immensely enjoyable and satisfying.

*U-TURNING IS OK IF IT'S OK*

*'At the time I consulted you I had been through a period when my heart wasn't in anything at all. I was chasing unsuitable positions and could not even convince myself, let alone any would-be employer. I was completely at sea. I came away from your interview in a very positive frame of mind, and with the overwhelming feeling that you had made me see what was important for me, and given me a firm sense of direction. Of course you had only shown me what was already there, but I was too blind at the time to recognize. Your recommendations involved my making a U-turn in my career, and you helped me to see this as a sign of strength rather than of failure. Without the boost you gave me, heaven only knows how much longer it might have been before I reached these sensible conclusions.'*

## Without Professional Career Guidance

If you can't afford to pay a career coach, and if you cannot find the right level of free guidance through one of the agencies listed in the Treasure Chest, you may have to rely on self-help. Here are some ideas you can try.

### The MAP Exercise

Turn to the Treasure Chest in Part 4 and use the MAP exercise there to try and get at your motivation, ability, and personality characteristics for yourself. Even if you do take professional career guidance this will be a useful exercise as it will help you reflect on and consolidate the advice you've been given. It will also be good preparation for the Quality of Match exercise which comes in Chapter 6 and looks at the match between you and your job.

## Self-Help Books

Try working out your motivation, ability, and personality from books. A visit to the psychology or management shelves of a good bookshop, or your local library, should help you find titles on testing your own motivation, aptitude, and personality.

## The Internet

If you have access to the internet there are hundreds of web sites offering all sorts of career information from psychometric testing to CV writing. Some are good, but most are not so good on guidance. Some require you to register with the site, others offer self-help tests. Some are free, most have a cost attached. So it's a matter of experimenting and using your judgement about what feels right for you. If you don't have your own computer you'll find free or cheap access computers in your local library.

To start looking use a search engine, typing in 'career assessment' or 'psychological tests'. This will present you with a very large number of relevant sites, but what is available for free is going to be quite limited. You certainly won't find a comprehensive analysis of your motivation, aptitude, and personality on any one site, although many sites offer more in-depth assessment for a fee. But such sites are useful if you want to see what psychometric tests look like, of if you want to practise test taking.

The internet is a useful source of information in helping you think about yourself and your career, but do exercise caution with self-help tests. Because no one is helping you interpret the tests in the context of yourself, don't be surprised if what you learn doesn't feel quite right. And most definitely don't let your life or your career be limited by information you feel is wrong for you.

## HOW DOES YOUR ARMOUR FIT?

I hope you can see now why self-awareness is an essential starter to any career journey, and why I call it the armour of protection. It's like looking through a telescope the wrong way round. You get an entirely different view. Most people look at what's out there in terms of careers, jobs, professions and wonder if they could fit. The right way is to look at yourself and then find ways of achieving your true potential. Keep working at it, though, because things change. Doing the MAP exercise is not a once for all thing that will last you a lifetime. It needs to be checked regularly.

In the language of Career Warrior you need to keep a constant check on your armour for goodness of fit. On a day to day basis it will probably be fine, but when it begins to feel uncomfortable start thinking about which bits need renewing.

## NEXT CHAPTER

Now that you have the armour of self-awareness to help protect you when things go wrong, work through Chapter 5 to acquire the weapons, or organizational skills, essential to managing your career.

It's a pick and choose chapter, so:

> Focus only on those skills most important to you in helping to overcome here and now problems.

> Learn by taking action.

> Leave the skills you don't need at present until you find you do need them.

# CHAPTER 5

> *Knowledge is a treasure, but practice is the key to it.*
>
> Thomas Fuller, *Gnomologia,* No 3139, c1650.

## WEAPONS FOR A CAREER WARRIOR

Now you're kitted out with the armour of self-knowledge you need some weapons to help you on your way. Weapons are useful for both defence and attack, and a range of different weapons is required for different situations.

For Career Warriors the weapons are organizational skills and the first problem is knowing what they are and how to find them. To manage your own career successfully it will be important to put together an armoury of skills. This could mean sharpening those you already have, but which have grown rusty, as well as searching for some new ones. It certainly means constant practice in using them until you become so expert they are second nature to you.

### BUILDING THE ARMOURY

In Chapter 2 we looked briefly at the weapons a Career Warrior needs. To remind you, here's the list again:

Self-Marketing

Networking

Organizational Politics

Interpersonal Skills

Proactivity

Creating Opportunities

Leadership

Stress Management

Action Learning

Each of these weapons is at your disposal in the Treasure Chest in Part 4. Lift the lid on them as and when you need them. But Action Learning, because it's such a powerful means of learning, has its own chapter (see Chapter 7).

The thing about weapons is you can read volumes about them but you'll only achieve full competence in using them through practical experience. It's exactly the same with career management skills. The more you practise using them the more skilled you'll become. And as your skills improve so will your confidence. As your confidence grows you'll feel more ready to use those skills to further your career. Suddenly, managing your own career – and doing it successfully – will become second nature.

What I want to encourage here is the idea of grasping the basics then getting on and learning from experience. So each of the Career Warrior weapons is described in sufficient outline to get you going. Don't try to memorize the whole list, and don't try to use them all at once. Start with those you need to get you moving on problems that are currently barriers in your career, your work, and your life.

For example, if you're finding difficulty getting people to go along with your ideas, start with Interpersonal Skills. Newly promoted but not getting a grip on your team? Begin with Leadership and Interpersonal Skills. If you feel overloaded by work, or trapped in a job you hate, look at Stress Management then move on to Creating Opportunities and Self-Marketing.

The point is you learn best when you are tackling real world problems that are part of your present day to day life. Of course the whole list of weapons is important but you can't gain instant skill in everything at once, so select the learning area you can put into practice right away and build up from there.

And don't worry that I've given you just the basics. They're distilled from years of experience as a leader, a manager, a trainer, a business consultant, and a career coach. They're designed to get you going so you can learn from experience in your own unique surroundings. If you want to expand your knowledge by learning more about the theory and background of the Career Warrior weapon skills you can do so by reading, by watching educational videos, or by going on a training course. But applying the basic skills to your real life problems will burn in the learning better than any other way.

**NEXT CHAPTER**

So what about when the armour and the weapons are not enough to overcome the really tough situations? Well that's when you have to live off your wits. Find out how to do this careerwise in the next chapter which reveals the art of career navigation – how to navigate your career through the fog of uncertainty.

# CHAPTER 6

> *They are ill discoverers that think there is no land, when all they can see is sea.*
>
> Francis Bacon, 1561-1626.

# THE WARRIOR'S WILES

## LATERAL THINKING

The Bible (1 Samuel, Chapter 17) tells us that when the mighty Philistine warrior Goliath challenged the Israelite army to present a man for single combat, David, a shepherd boy, stepped forward. Although completely outclassed by the superior armour and weapons of Goliath, David saved the day for the Israelites by felling the giant with a stone hurled from his sling.

This is a fine example of lateral thinking, or being creative when the problem seems impossible to solve. And, like David, the Career Warrior must develop the wiles, or the art of lateral thinking, to combat those situations where armour and weapons are not in themselves enough to win the day.

If life was simple you'd work out your self-identity using the MAP idea of Chapter 4 and then look for a career role that formed an identical match with your motivation, ability, and personality. Great if you can do it, but unfortunately life is about reality. Remember the bit about people and situations constantly changing? As economic and social life changes, so do organizations and job roles, and often the way we live. Think of how things like shopping, travel, and communication have changed and affected our jobs and our lives.

And if you're making a first career choice, or changing career, or even just changing who you work for, there are new skills to learn, new ways of doing things, new managers to please. Even if you stay where you are, nothing is fixed.

So it becomes important to manage your long-term career by having a clear idea of what your long-term career direction is, and how you can best use your present situation to help steer you towards your goals. This means being in control of and planning your career. We call this process career navigation.

By the way, looking after yourself doesn't mean neglecting your present job or your employer's needs – quite the contrary. It's through the practical experience of meeting the challenges of work that you'll acquire the Career Warrior's weapons – the organizational skills listed in the previous chapter that you need to master if you're going to manage your own career successfully. We spend a great part of our waking lives at work – whatever our work is and regardless of whether we like it – so why not take advantage of it to hone your career management skills?

## THE PROCESS OF CAREER NAVIGATION

We need to develop this skill because modern organizational life, and indeed life itself, is filled with uncertainty. Self-awareness is our armour because it gives us protection when the life storms generated through uncertainty make us feel we are out of tune with our career role. Sound knowledge of self allows us to understand what is happening to us in terms of mismatch between our self-identity and the situation. Thus we avoid the panic, stress, loss of self-confidence, and weakened self-esteem that comes from seeing ourselves rather than the situation as the problem.

The idea is to use knowledge of the armour of self-awareness as a navigation instrument to help us make judgements about career situation, and decisions about career choice, by using understanding of our motivation, ability, and personality to weigh organizational opportunities and threats. This helps us see short-term career issues in the broader perspective of our long-term future.

The way to achieve balance is to think laterally – to look for ways to change the situation so we have a better match with our self-identity instead of trying to force ourselves to become a match with a role that is wrong for us. So career navigation is about navigating your career through the fog of organizational and life uncertainty, using self-awareness as the navigation instrument.

It may happen, and frequently does, that despite our best efforts it's not possible to improve the quality of match between self and job. If this is you, and if you can change jobs, move to another that's a better match. If you cannot change jobs then the career navigation task is about managing the mismatch between the MAP of your self-identity and the MAP of your work or life role. At least you'll be able to identify the mismatch and know what it is you have to manage. That way you stay in control. The alternative is to let the situation control you – a sure way to demotivation and unhappiness – and very likely to workplace stress.

Useful to keep in mind as you work through this process are the words of Francis Bacon given in the chapter quotation. Just because you can't see a solution at present it doesn't mean there isn't one out there. So practise the skill of career navigation until it becomes an automatic response.

*PUSHING HIS MAP THE WRONG WAY PUT STAN IN HOSPITAL*

*An excellent information technologist, Stan was happy with his research and development work. He loved analyzing data and he enjoyed the predictable and structured world of facts and figures (motivation). His strongest aptitude was for logical reasoning and analysis, and the backroom nature of his work suited his quiet temperament (personality).*

*Because he was so good at his job he was given a managerial role. Stan didn't want it and asked to be left to do the work he loved. When his line manager insisted, Stan asked at least for a trial period shadowing his current boss to give him confidence. His request was not granted and he was in at the deep end. Having to focus on people management was totally against Stan's strongest motivation, his best aptitude, and his personality style. Stan struggled, but because he was a conscientious man he tried hard to make himself fit the role.*

*Some months later Stan suffered a breakdown at work and spent several months in hospital. When he returned to work after a long absence he was offered career coaching which revealed both the mismatch between his self-identity and the managerial role and his strong match with research and development work.*

*Fortunately, Stan's head of department was a sympathetic and understanding person willing to listen. With a clear picture of why things had gone wrong, Stan was allowed to return to his original role where he was not only content and happy but considerably more effective and of much greater value to his organization.*

## THE MATCHING PROCESS IN PICTURES

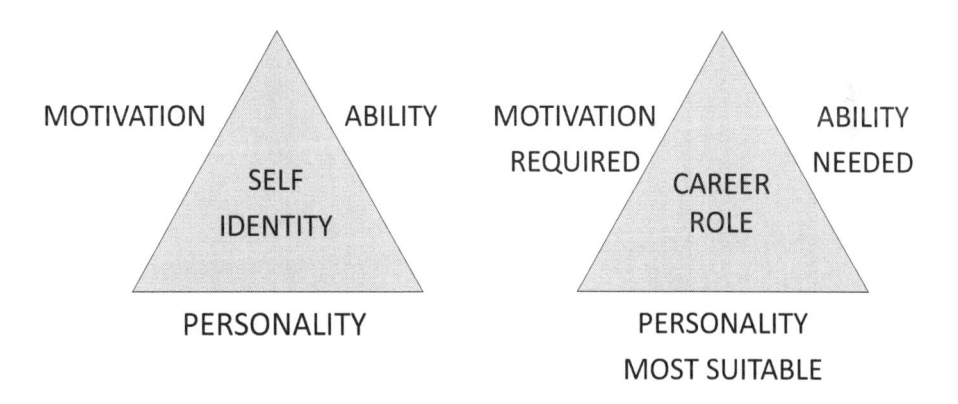

```
       MOTIVATION   ABILITY          MOTIVATION         ABILITY
                                     REQUIRED           NEEDED
            SELF                           CAREER
          IDENTITY                          ROLE

           PERSONALITY                   PERSONALITY
                                        MOST SUITABLE
```

Just as every individual possesses certain characteristics of motivation, ability, and personality so every career role can be described in terms of the kind of motivation required to really want to do that kind of work, the level of ability needed to be successful at it, and the qualities of personality that would make a person feel happy and comfortable in the role. Career navigation is about seeking the best degree of fit between the two.

## An Ideal Match

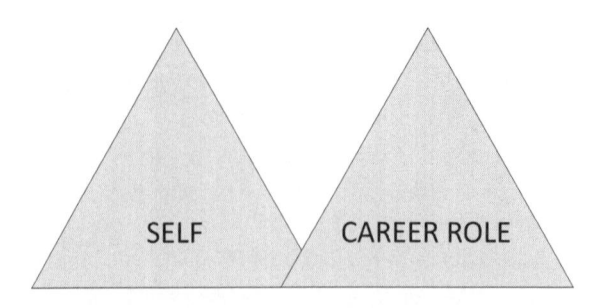

Here the person has found a career role perfectly matched to their motivation, their ability, and their personality. This is tough to achieve, especially since the world around us and we ourselves are constantly changing. Really it's an ideal to aim for, so you may get close then lose some of the match and then get close again. Be sure about this though. When you master the skill of career navigation to the point where you approach your ideal you will achieve a level of job satisfaction and fulfilment that will astound you.

## A Mismatch

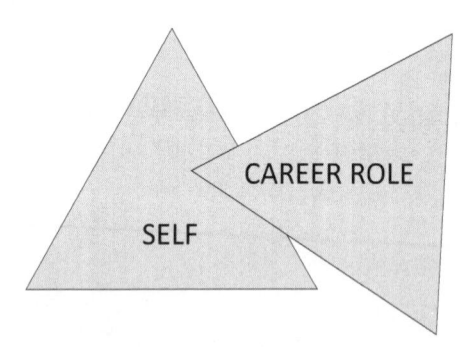

In this situation the person and the job have some degree of mismatch because motivation, ability, and personality are not closely aligned. Maybe this person has found a role for which they have good qualifications (ability), and in which they feel well suited to the people and the organization (personality), but where the work lacks the kind of challenge they are seeking (motivation). Or maybe motivation, ability, and personality matches are reasonable to a degree but insufficient to satisfy the individual's needs.

A great many people find themselves in this situation. In fact probably the majority of people I've worked with on career coaching fit this description. They know things are not quite right but they can't put a finger on why. They use language like, 'I feel out of tune with my work' or 'I know things are wrong but I don't know why'. Another comment I hear often is, 'I know what I don't like about my job but I don't know what I want'. The mismatch brings a vague feeling of all not being well, and very often this can be a career danger area because if the uncertainty becomes strong it can lead to feelings of being out of control. And feeling out of control usually ends up as some kind of work stress.

When people experience this kind of mismatch they frequently blame themselves. Believing they must have some kind of failing, they struggle to push their MAP triangle round to make a better match with the job, in the process distorting their self-identity and losing sight of who they really are. The outcome is usually a great deal of distress and unhappiness – the career confusion I referred to as the Snowstorm Effect in Chapter 4.

But when we understand the idea of self-identity, become self-aware, and use the language of motivation, ability, and personality we can see career problems clearly. The right thing to do of course is to have a sound understanding of the mismatch and to try and bring the job MAP round to become a match with the self-identity MAP. People often say it's not possible to do that because their line manager or their organization gives them no freedom. Sadly this may be true, but so often people who thought they couldn't make a difference to their working lives actually succeed in doing so once they understand the problem and make up their mind to do something about it.

The secret is in understanding the interaction between self and job and taking responsibility for managing the situation. And even if you're unlucky enough to be in a job where nobody will listen to you or help you, just being aware of these ideas about career navigation is helpful because you will understand the problem is in the mismatch with your job and not in yourself.

## JUST KNOWING WAS ENOUGH

*Wendy hated with a passion her job as a data entry clerk in a large insurance company. Tied to a computer screen all day, she described her life as like being in a long black tunnel with no light at the end. Eventually she became ill at the thought of having to go to work and was prescribed medication by her GP to help her cope.*

*Career coaching showed Wendy to be a warm and caring person (personality) who longed to give a personal service to people (motivation). Her strongest aptitude was for practical work with people. In discussion Wendy recalled wanting to be a nurse when she was at school.*

*A career change into nursing would have been an ideal move but Wendy was a single parent with young children and needed the money her current job brought. The interesting aspect of this case was that just knowing she was ideally suited to nursing, and that her present problems were a result of a mismatch with the job rather than a failing in herself, made her feel much better.*

*As is often the case when this kind of insight occurs Wendy sobbed with relief and understanding. She now felt better able to cope with the data entry work because she had clarity about why she felt the way she did. She still felt as though she was in a dark tunnel but now she could see some light in the form of the possibility of moving into nursing when the children were older.*

*Meanwhile we discussed the idea of a couple of hours' hospital visiting on a Sunday and maybe an evening course in health care at the local college when she could find a regular child minder.*

*Wendy returned to work feeling better, and with a vision of a future that brought light into the dark moments.*

## Disaster Potential

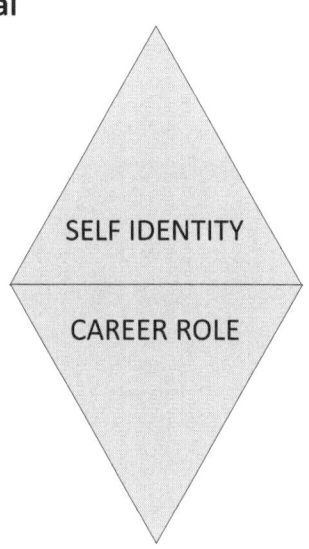

```
     SELF IDENTITY
     ─────────────
     CAREER ROLE
```

The worst kind of mismatch is when self-identity and the job are totally out of tune in all directions. I know because it happened to me; I was able to make sense of it only by looking backward over my life after I had made career management my specialist field of study. In fact one of the major reasons for developing and writing about Career Warrior is that I want to use my knowledge and experience to help people who may find themselves in a similar situation.

At the time I lived and worked in this scenario I was an engineer. I disliked intensely the practical aspects of engineering (motivation), I could never understand more than the most elementary engineering principles and had abysmal hand skills (ability), and machines and engineering talk left me cold (personality). I felt completely out of tune with technology, saw myself as pretty incompetent, and constantly waited for the day when I'd be unmasked as a fraud. I recall passing my engineering examinations by memorizing theory and drawings, and then forgetting everything the moment the exam was over.

By accident, because I hadn't studied psychology then, I survived by pulling the job MAP round to me rather than trying to push my MAP round to the job. In fact I did quite well by becoming a manager and leading and motivating the real engineers who were brilliant at managing the technology.

The point of this story is that even when the match between you and your job is at its worst you can survive, and even prosper, if you understand the mismatch and manage it appropriately. But one thing I know for sure – you learn to cope but you never feel truly easy and comfortable in there. And it certainly isn't the place to find your sense of fulfilment in life.

As I now know, my motivation is about helping, guiding, and advising people. My best aptitude is for learning, communicating, and problem solving with people, and my practical engineering incompetence is down to having very little spatial and mechanical aptitude. My personality is highly people centred. It was studying psychology with the Open University that first gave me an educated insight into these kind of relationships between people and work, and which led me to make a career change into psychology. In this profession I feel I've found the ideal match. Now, I've never felt happier and more fulfilled in my work.

## CHECKING YOUR QUALITY OF MATCH

Take a look in the Treasure Chest in Part 4 and use the Checking The Quality Of Match exercise there to check your career navigation. Or maybe use the exercise to weigh up how well you match your dream job. And if you do, well, why not go for it? If you truly want it you can have it.

## NAVIGATING TOWARDS THE DREAM JOB

The Quality of Match exercise will have given you some clues about yourself and the kind of work that suits you. Armed with these ideas, and the words you've used to describe them, now look at the vast range of career options. Many of them you won't even have heard of.

There are dozens of books that give information on different careers, but probably the best place to start is with your national careers service. In the UK, for example, on the national careers website you'll find over 750 job profiles containing comprehensive careers information including:

- Job descriptions
- The kind of work involved
- The work environment
- Skills and interests needed
- Entry requirements
- Training and development
- Pay and conditions
- Prospects
- Contact details for further information
- Recommended reading on that career

If you can't find the information you're looking for, contact the service and speak to an adviser (contact details for the UK, Scottish, and Welsh services are in the Treasure Chest). Alternatively, or if you aren't a resident of those nations, study the UK website then visit your local library and ask a librarian to help you find information on the career area of interest to you.

Now turn that thinking into action by contacting people already employed in the career field in which you're interested. Ask them if you can come for a short networking visit to talk about their work because you're interested in it as a career for yourself. You might get some rejections, but more often than not people are keen to talk about their work and what they do. Believe me, I've seen it work successfully many times.

## NEXT CHAPTER

The next chapter takes us into Part 3 which describes how to make career self-management work. You have the armour and the weapons, and you understand the principles of how to navigate your career (the wiles). The next three chapters are about keeping your career quest alive and on track.

Chapter 7 describes in detail how to go about forming and managing a self-help Action Learning group. All you need is to find a few like minded people. Trust me, if you're able to do this you'll find it the most powerful learning experience you'll ever encounter.

If you aren't able to make this work do read through the chapter anyway as you'll find useful tips to help you with your career planning. You'll also see how Action Learning may be useful at work and in other areas of your life.

# PART 3

## The Journey And The Quest

### Finding the way and following the pioneers

# CHAPTER 7

> *I keep six honest serving men*
> *(They taught me all I knew);*
> *Their names are What and Why and When*
> *And How and Where and Who.*
>
> Rudyard Kipling, *The Elephant's Child,* 1902.

## ACTION LEARNING – AND HOW TO MAKE IT WORK

### SEVERAL HEADS ARE BETTER THAN ONE

There's absolutely no doubt that your career self-management will be significantly more effective if you make the effort to work together with a few people who are also interested in taking responsibility for the management of their own career. Fellow Career Warriors who want to follow their career quest in company. The best way to do this is by setting up an Action Learning group. It's simple. You can do it by using this chapter as your guide.

Ask around to find a few people who are interested in developing their career and willing to commit about four hours a fortnight to meeting up together, and a few hours each week to doing things for themselves. Ideally, an Action Learning group has five people but it will work well enough with four or six. Less than four makes the group too small for best effect. Beyond six it tends to be too big for smooth running.

But don't be put off if you can't get these numbers right. One of the great strengths of Action Learning is its flexibility. It's a process, not a structure, so what's most important is how you do it, and how you interact with your colleagues when you meet for a working session.

## SO WHERE DID ACTION LEARNING COME FROM?

You don't need to know this to do Action Learning successfully, but if you never touch base with the writing and work of Reg Revans – the father of Action Learning – you miss a wonderful opportunity to understand the thinking behind what is, in my long experience of management development and training, the most powerful adult learning method I've encountered. It will exceed all your expectations if you commit to it.

It's neither clever nor necessary to embellish much of what Revans has said because his teaching is simple and basic. It's this very simplicity that accounts for the longevity of Action Learning as a problem solving and personal development tool. So almost all that's written in this chapter draws on the work and writing of that great man.

### REG REVANS

*Whilst Professor Reg Revans has always been quick to point out he didn't actually invent Action Learning, frequently by drawing attention to examples of it in the Old Testament of the Christian Bible and in the teachings of Buddha, there are few who would not attribute its growth to him.*

*Born in 1907, and active in the University of Salford Revans Institute for Action Learning and Research until shortly before his death at the age of 95, Reg's influence has spread across the world. Tributes to his work range from the award of Belgium's Order of Leopold to recognition in Eastern management textbooks of his influence on Japanese management techniques.*

*A 1928 Olympic athlete at the age of 21 and a Cambridge research fellow in physics at 25, Reg was steeped in both learning and activity.*

*Moving into education at age 28, Reg was appointed Higher Education Assistant for Essex County Council, and in the early post World War Two years became Director of Education for the National Coal Board. So it's possible to see the organizational management origins of Action Learning in the 1940s.*

*To learn more about Reg Revans and his work read his book The ABC of Action Learning, first published in 1978 but more recently republished by Gower Publishing (2011).*

## AND WHAT IS ACTION LEARNING?

In Action Learning we try to avoid tight definitions because as soon as you define something you put boundaries around it and limit its flexibility. The only way really to know about Action Learning is to do it and learn from the experience. But you need to have some idea of where you're going before you start the journey so here's a simple starter explanation:

***A small group of people who choose to meet on a regular basis to learn from each other by sharing their ideas and challenging each other on their thinking.***

When I launch a new Action Learning group I give each participant a newsletter I've put together over the years which answers a lot of questions people have when they first start Action Learning. I call it *Super Trouper* after the follow spot searchlight used in theatres because I'm putting the spotlight on Action Learning. You'll find a copy of *Super Trouper* in the Treasure Chest in Part 4.

Action Learning is both a problem solving forum and an adult learning process, and by tradition we call such a group a set. Armed with that simple information you can form your own Action learning set and learn as you go. But you'll not be doing Action Learning unless you follow two basic principles which are at its heart: challenging questioning and managing a project.

### *Challenging Questioning*
Asking questions that challenge thinking is a powerful learning process.

It helps the person being asked because it forces them to explain their thinking in a way that helps others understand the reasoning behind what they're saying. Having to explain your thoughts in detail, especially to a persistent questioner, encourages you to clarify your thinking.

It helps the person asking the question because it enables them to fill a gap in their knowledge and understanding.

It helps those who are listening because their learning benefits from the questioning and answering. And listening to questions often triggers reflection on their own issues.

With experience we learn the art of asking really challenging questions. Look at this chapter's quotation. It contains six excellent first words to a challenging question, perhaps the most powerful of which is Why. A series of Why questions helps us peel back the layers of uncertainty to get to the core of a problem because it challenges us to think very carefully about why we do what we do.

But even simple questions can be productive. Here's a real life example from an organization I worked with. It started in the office.

### THE POWER OF ASKING QUESTIONS

*Q. Why do we spend so much time gathering statistics to send to headquarters in our monthly report?*

*A. I don't know. We've always done it.*

*The next question was a telephone call to headquarters.*

*Q. Why do you want these statistics from us?*

*A. We don't. You've sent them for as long as I can remember so we thought you must have a reason. But we don't use them.*

You can guess the outcome – and the savings in time and paper!

The point of challenging questioning is to learn. So we don't try to trip people up, we don't cause offence, and we don't take offence at being questioned. We avoid conflict in our questioning because conflict produces winners and losers. Creating the kind of environment in which we can do this takes time and patience because we have to generate mutual trust and understanding, so don't expect to be skilled at challenging questioning too soon.

Ultimately it's only by being truly open to the questioning of set colleagues, and by reflecting on their questioning, that we gain true insight to our problems – and more importantly true insight to ourselves. Mark, a newcomer to Action Learning, said this about his first set meeting:

> 'I joined an Action Learning set at a time when I realized my job wasn't really ever going to work out properly. With the support of my set colleagues I was able to articulate a critique of my position and the difficulties I had with my work, and through insightful questioning they helped me confirm my analysis was correct. This was the first time I had been able to do this without fear of offending a whole series of managers, or just sounding like a whinging troublemaker. Crucially, it was the first time I'd been able to feel I could make something happen about it.
>
> I left my first set meeting with a much more powerful sense of what I was good at, what I enjoyed doing in my work, and an almost overwhelming sense that I would no longer make do with cruddy compromises in order to stay safe. After a couple of days' reflection on this first meeting I became somewhat "high", not only because of how the Action Learning process had worked for me, but because of the open, honest, and caring questioning and listening that went on throughout the day. Although it took a while to process, you could say I came in with the power of one person and left feeling like I had the power of six.'

### *Managing A Project*

People learn best when they engage in some purposeful activity. By purposeful we mean something of significant importance in their work or their lives. For example, it could be something to do with a problem at work, a community initiative, a voluntary or charitable commitment, their own personal development, something they want to achieve but don't know how to begin.

The problem or the issue becomes the Action Learning project, and the project becomes the vehicle for learning through experience. We take action to move the project forward and we learn from the experience of doing that. New learning enables new action and the new action produces more new learning. So the process of Action Learning continues and grows.

We choose to work on real life issues because simulations and games don't carry the same level of personal involvement. It's the struggle to overcome real world barriers that leads to insightful learning about the world and, more importantly, to knowledge about ourselves.

Of course we can learn the theory of how things are done in the classroom or training room, but it's the activity of having to tackle each stage of problem solving in a real world environment that helps us consolidate that learning in a way we're unlikely to forget. As many wise people have observed, knowing how is not the same as doing.

An Action Learning set provides exactly the right environment for this kind of learning because the same group of people meet together over a period of time, gradually forming friendships and bonds which encourage an atmosphere of mutual trust and support.

In this atmosphere we can challenge our thinking and our behaviour in a non threatening way that leads to new learning, and eventually to the solution of our particular problem. We do this by questioning the thinking and the ideas of our colleagues, and by supporting them. We don't try to solve anybody's problem for them because that prevents them from learning from experience. We just help them to know what's right for them.

Managing a project and challenging questioning are core ingredients essential to successful Action Learning. They're the strong pillars that support the arch of your learning and development. Regularly check out with your Action Learning set colleagues that you're accomplishing both. Here's Mark again:

> 'By chance a former collaborator asked me if I would be interested in a new project. Vague and interesting just about defined the whole set up – but armed

*with the knowledge about myself the set had reflected back at me I felt able to accept the challenge. I was questioned about the new position, and it just confirmed that the whole thing was right. More than that, I knew then (and it's turned out) that my set colleagues would be there to support me through the challenges ahead and elicit from me answers to the questions my new role would pose. I don't get direct answers to the issues I bring to the set, but I am challenged and encouraged to answer their questions from my perspective, in my situation, and in my style. Now, as a project manager who has learned from the techniques used in Action Learning, my set participation strengthens not just me but my whole project and my team.'*

## LETS GO THEN

We have five like-minded people, now we need a place to meet. It does need to be a private place because sooner or later you'll get round to private stuff. It's not essential, but if you can find someone experienced in Action Learning to act as group facilitator it will help you get on the road more quickly. If you have no suitable facilitator don't worry, you can do it for yourself by following this chapter – it's just likely to take a little longer to get used to it.

In any case any decent facilitator will get out of your hair as quickly as possible. The facilitator, called the set adviser in Action Learning, is not a member of your Action Learning set. She or he is there solely to help the set discover how to engage in Action Learning as a means of managing and solving their particular problems and issues. The wise set adviser will leave you long before you're experienced Action Learning practitioners, but not before you've grasped the essentials of how to conduct set meetings. The whole point is you learn by doing it.

If you do feel the need for a facilitator try an internet Google search for Action Learning set adviser. You should be able to find someone in your region, but do be aware that the facilitator will charge for the service.

So five, possibly six if you've found a set adviser, are sitting around a table. Where do we go from here? The first meeting should be about getting to know each other, making sure you have some shared ideas of what Action Learning is about, and constructing a framework for action you can all commit to.

There's no one right way – you work out what's right for you. But:

> The two principles of asking challenging questions and having a project are the core components that make Action Learning work.
>
> You always own your own problem and accept responsibility for it.
>
> We don't aim to solve people's problems for them. We help them find their own solutions.

We don't have agendas and minutes of meetings. Action Learning is not about generating paper, it's about asking questions and taking action. Of course there will be some paper, such as contact address lists for example, but we try to keep it to an absolute minimum. It's important, though, that each set member should keep a learning log to record the progress of their learning (see Chapter 8 on keeping a learning journal).

Here's one way of launching an Action Learning set. I use it when I'm acting as a set adviser and have developed it through experience. Timings are a guideline only and can be adjusted to suit your own situation. The short breaks are important because they're valuable as thinking time and give participants an opportunity to swap thoughts and ideas, itself a useful learning tool. After the example I explain briefly what each activity is about.

### INTRODUCTION TO ACTION LEARNING

| | |
|---|---|
| *Break the ice with introductions* | *30 mins* |
| *Each participant says something about themself, what they do, and why they've joined the set* | |
| *Dump session* | *15 mins* |

| | |
|---|---|
| *Explain the role of the set adviser* | *5 mins* |
| *Explain what Action Learning is* <br> *(two basic principles of challenging questioning* <br> *and having a project)* | *20 mins* |
| *Break* | *15 mins* |
| *Set some basic ground rules* | *20 mins* |
| *Discuss expectations* | *20 mins* |
| *Experiment with Action Learning* | *30 mins* |
| *Break* | *15 mins* |
| *Set diary dates* | *15 mins* |
| *Bullet points on learning* | *10 mins* |
| *Sound off* | *20 mins* |

## Introductions

No pressure. A gentle introduction to give everyone a voice.

## Dump Session

The start of a habit for the beginning of every set meeting in the future. Going around the table each person spends no more than two minutes saying how they feel today and dumping any irritations. This is definitely not question and answer time. The purpose is to enable people, for the duration of the meeting, to park things that are niggling at their mind so they can give their undivided attention to group work.

Examples might be 'couldn't find a car park so got here late', 'had a row with the boss this morning and still feel angry', 'got a violent headache and feel rotten'. Just telling someone often helps people offload things, at least temporarily, so they can concentrate better in the meeting.

### Explain The Role Of The Set Adviser

To help the set move quickly into Action Learning mode. The set adviser, if you have one, is not part of the set and will leave it at the earliest possible point. This will probably be after three to six meetings, but the exact point of departure will depend on how the set is operating. If you don't have a set adviser there's enough information in this guide to help you get going.

### Explain What Action Learning Is

Use the explanations given in this chapter together with the information in *Super Trouper* (see the Treasure Chest in Part 4). It would be a good idea to make copies of *Super Trouper* for each member of the set. Alternatively use bits and pieces from *Super Trouper* to design your own newsletter. But remember we don't give tight definitions because you learn about Action Learning by doing it.

### Set Some Basic Ground Rules

We try to avoid too much administration in Action Learning. Definitely no agendas or minutes. But it's useful to have some common agreement about the way we behave if our set is to be effective. I often use the term guidelines for responsible behaviour instead of ground rules.

The set discusses and decides its own ground rules. It's helpful to ask for a volunteer to write down the ground rules and make copies for the other set members because it quickly creates involvement in the Action Learning process. Here are some ground rules sets tend to agree on.

GUIDELINES FOR RESPONSIBLE BEHAVIOUR IN OUR SET

*Meetings start on time and finish on time*

*If you can't make the meeting let someone know*

*No external interruptions. Mobile phones switched off*

*We all commit to every meeting*

*Each set member has equal status at set meetings*

*Maintain confidentiality of set discussion*

*Every question and idea is worthy of discussion*

*Don't give offence, don't take offence*

*Give honest feedback with empathy and tact*

*Every speaker gets 100 per cent attention from the set*

*Guidelines can be changed any time by set agreement*

These are examples taken from a number of sets. Yours will be different. You don't have to have groundrules if you don't want them. It's up to you. But they will help your set to keep working smoothly.

## *Discuss Expectations*

It helps if everyone in the set has some idea of what the others are looking to gain from being part of the set. If you have access to a flip chart invite a set member to use it for recording points raised; if not, get somebody to write the points down. Ask for a volunteer to copy the list of points and send the list to each member of the set. If forming the set is your idea, try to avoid doing these simple tasks yourself because you need to help your colleagues feel involved as early as possible. This will also encourage commitment to the long-term future of the set.

## *Experiment With Action Learning*

In an introductory programme it's useful to run a brief Action Learning taster session to reinforce the ideas under discussion and to try out the method. A volunteer who has in mind a problem of work, career, or life they are willing to share with the set should state their problem simply, say in less than one minute, and then allow the other set members to question them about it for about ten minutes. Use the challenging questions method as described earlier.

Depending on time available, run one or more of these brief taster sessions before going on to diary dates. After each session spend five minutes discussing how it felt for everyone.

### Set Diary Dates

Agree dates when all set members are available. The further ahead you plan your dates the easier it's going to be to find spaces in the diaries of busy people. And it will be useful at this meeting to plan for at least the following six months. Again you're working at generating commitment to the set.

### Bullet Points On Learning

The start of another habit which should be introduced towards the end of every Action Learning set meeting. Allocate a little quiet time for individual reflection on what's been learned from the meeting. Set members write down two or three bullet points, or short notes, summarizing their learning and which they later transfer to their personal learning record. Over time these learning points will become a valuable log of personal development. For more on keeping a learning journal see Chapter 8.

### Sound Off

Another good habit for all set meetings. Much set activity is about the discussion of facts related to participants' problems. So it's not a bad idea to round off the meeting with a time slot for people to say how they feel about the meeting. Very often how we feel about something gets in the way of how we interpret and act on facts.

Remember this is a guide based on my experience of launching several Action Learning sets, but it's only a guide. You don't have to do it this way or stick to the timings suggested. Do it your way.

Even if you have a set adviser, getting people to do things – such as writing on flip charts and copying lists for other set members – is beneficial for all because it starts the process of taking responsibility for their own future.

> 'Although I felt very challenged at times, for me this way of working always pointed to the real action needed: I can't think of another approach to learning that I've experienced which has both brought me so much insight to tackle my own work-related issues and enabled me to help others in a similar way.
>
> From my experience I would say that provided care is taken in the early development of the set, then Action Learning is an excellent way for set members to draw on each other's expertise and support for both personal and professional development.'
>
> Jane

## THE ACTION LEARNING SET MEETING

The introductory session is necessary to help people understand what the process of Action Learning is about. It's the framework on which the set will build and develop their skills, knowledge, and attitude as they work through a Career Warrior programme using Action Learning as the vehicle for their development.

But from now on you can devote the whole of each meeting to Action Learning. How you structure your set meetings is up to you as a group, but here are some ideas you can use as a guide. Dump session, bullet points, and sound off were described in the previous section so need no further explanation.

STRUCTURE FOR A HALF DAY SET MEETING

| | |
|---|---|
| Dump session | 15 mins |
| Manage time | 15 mins |
| 1$^{st}$ and 2$^{nd}$ speaker | 30 mins each |
| Break | 15 mins |
| 3$^{rd}$ and 4th speaker | 30 mins each |

| | |
|---|---:|
| *Break* | *15 mins* |
| *5th speaker* | *30 mins* |
| *Bullet points on learning* | *10 mins* |
| *Sound off* | *20 mins* |

## Manage Time

Discuss how set members feel about who should speak and in what order. Some people may feel more anxious about wanting to discuss their issues early in the meeting. Others may prefer to wait until nearer the end of the session.

Sometimes a set member may feel they need an extended time slot because they've a particularly difficult problem to air. Or someone may feel they've little to talk about and would rather not take up their time slot. These things should be agreed by all so there's no misunderstanding about who gets to speak and for how long.

## Speakers

There's no fixed time: 30 minutes is an example of what I've found to be reasonable. Nor does everyone need to speak if the set chooses to do it some other way.

My advice, though, particularly in the earlier meetings when the set is beginning to explore the ideas behind Action Learning, is to split the time available for speaking equally between set members. There are several reasons for this:

> The quieter members of the set aren't always good at speaking up for what they want.
>
> The more confident set members are good at taking up more than a fair share of time.

Some people will put their own needs to one side because they have a conviction that other people's needs are greater than theirs.

Taking a turn at speaking is a good way to help people develop the time management skills needed for effective set meetings.

Often a set member feels they have nothing to say, but when given air time and questioned about their project some useful learning usually arises.

### Dividing Up Your Time As Speaker

When it comes to your turn to speak it's up to you how you manage your air time. There are, however, some important points to consider. The most important part of a set meeting is the process of getting colleagues to challenge your thinking, so most of your time slot should be given up to this.

Beware the common fault of spending too much of your time talking. If you're talking you aren't listening. Think about what you are going to say before you come to the meeting so you can state your issue or problem as briefly as possible and move on to the questioning phase where you'll find the help you need in tackling your issue.

As you listen to the questions that come up jot down anything that feels like a learning point or a new idea. This will help you in feeding back to your colleagues how their questions have helped you.

It's important to learn by taking action, so you need to allocate space at the end of your air time to state what action you will take before the next set meeting so your colleagues can help you maintain the balance between your action and your learning.

Here's a guideline for dividing up speaking time which I've used over many years and found to work well. But do change it if it doesn't suit your set.

| | |
|---|---|
| 2 mins | State the issue or problem you want to discuss today |
| 25 mins | Colleagues ask questions |
| 3 mins | Summarize what you've learned from the questioning and state what action you will take before the next set meeting |

## Tracking Time Across The Action Learning Set Meeting

Initially the set adviser, if you have one, will take care of overall timing and gradually help the set to manage time for itself. If you're meeting without a set adviser you'll need to agree some way of keeping track of time through the session. You'll soon find that keeping time is a highly troublesome activity.

Timing is important if the Action Learning set is to operate effectively. If you're allocated 30 minutes and speak for 45 minutes you've cheated someone else out of time they may be counting on to air their problem. And overall, if five set members feel a need to speak it's important that none is robbed of the chance to do so by bad timekeeping.

## Time To Explore

As the group grows in confidence it will not be necessary for each set member to have equal air time at every meeting. And now and again it'll be important to allocate some time to group discussion of issues of common concern. For example:

>What are we doing here?

>Are we actually doing Action Learning? (see How do you know you are Action Learning? in *Super Trouper* in the Treasure Chest in Part 4).

>Do we see the time we devote to Action Learning as productive and useful?

As time goes by and set members become more experienced and skilled at Action Learning there are likely to be occasions when questioning centres on you and your behaviour in relation to the problem you've brought to the meeting. This can feel scary at first, but if questioning can be done without giving or taking offence it's a wonderful route to self-awareness. In Career Warrior language you'll be strengthening your protective armour.

> 'Although I'd been on an introductory day about the Action Learning approach I really had very little idea of how powerful it could be in practice. And although my learning background had included formal stuff like degrees as well as informal stuff like workshop based courses, not to mention having taught both children and adults myself for several years, this managed to feel utterly new.
>
> It's certainly been the most powerful learning method that I've ever experienced. I have found it challenging in a way that none of the above ever felt. And working with other people from their own experiences feels real, useful and – irritating word – empowering.
>
> There seems to be a particular value in coming together with the same people time and again; whether it depends on the particular group of people I don't know. The days are intense, hard work, exhausting and energizing at the same time. It works for me on a whole load of levels – practical, intellectual, emotional.'
>
> Amanda

## WHY ACTION LEARNING SETS FAIL

Sometimes Action Learning sets do stop working effectively. Set members become bored or unhappy with the process and stop coming to meetings. 'Lost the plot' is quite a good term to use here because I've found from experience that what's happened is loss of the basic Action Learning process.

### *Time Management*

Time management can be very difficult to master. Given 30 minutes to talk, people completely lose track of time as they immerse themselves in their particular issue or problem. Others in the group either don't watch the time at all or are reluctant to mention it. This means less time for someone else or, worse, for the last to speak, no time at all. Resentment can set in even if the issue isn't raised. And planned breaks can be skipped – a really bad idea as people need some space to recharge their batteries before the next speaker. Or breaks go on so long they take up the next speaker's time slot.

Time management might sound like a trivial matter but, particularly during the early stages of a set's life, it's crucial to happy and effective set meetings. You will learn the skills of timing as the set progresses, but in the early days poor timing could lead to set failure.

## Lack Of Commitment

Every set member needs to show commitment to the work of the set by their presence at set meetings. Obviously there are going to be times when it really is impossible to be there, but these apart, the work of the set should be so important and so valuable that meetings become an essential part of work or life routine. If it doesn't feel like this it's time to look at what's going on in set meetings. When people drop out too easily it becomes a habit. Others follow suit and the set crumbles.

When Action Learning is working well the set meeting becomes unmissable because the level of learning is so high for the time involved it becomes the most productive means of development in a person's life.

## The Lost Q

There's a danger that over time the whole point of Action Learning – the challenging questioning – is lost as the set becomes cosy and gossip oriented. The dump session extends and becomes a lengthy conversation about all the social activity since the last meeting. Talking about work issues and problems to be overcome becomes an offload session of all the ills surrounding the history of the problem and a repeat of much that's been said before.

There's nothing wrong with doing this, and I know people find it comforting, but it isn't Action Learning. Action Learning is problem focused, and to be effective meetings should be businesslike and centred on the core essentials of managing your issues and being open to challenging questioning about them. The way to revitalize wilting set meetings is to restore the challenge of insightful questioning. Without that the set loses direction and purpose as a forum for action and learning.

If people do have a need for social conversation arrange to meet earlier, or stay later, or fix a chat session. But don't confuse it with Action Learning.

## NEXT CHAPTER

Whether you work on your personal development alone, or together with others in an Action Learning set, making a record of your learning will help you reinforce it and keep track of it.

Read Chapter 8 to discover why it's important to write down your thoughts, and how to go about it in a structured way that will bring you considerable career benefits.

# CHAPTER 8

> *Learning is but an adjunct to ourself and where we are our learning likewise is.*
>
> William Shakespeare, *Love's Labour's Lost,* Act iv, Sc iii.

# KEEPING A LEARNING JOURNAL – CAREER AS A STORY

## THE BENEFITS OF HINDSIGHT

If you had a friendly wizard who could grant you a magic wish, wouldn't it be useful to be able to visit the future and look back over your life? You'd have all the wisdom that comes with experience and all the knowledge gained from your successes and your mistakes. Then, once the wizard had whisked you back to the present, you could use that wisdom and knowledge to navigate your career and your life so that you avoid the pitfalls you'd seen looking back. You'd have the story of your life to use as a guide.

Career Warrior is the outcome of me looking back over the story of my life and writing it down so I could pick out the learning from it. Unfortunately I don't have a wizard who can take me back for another go, but what I've learned in my lifetime will be useful to those who don't have a friendly wizard to help them see their future. Remember the old saying there's no substitute for experience? Well that may be true, but nobody said the experience has to be your own.

Of course my experience won't be the same as your experience so use Career Warrior as a guide to help you avoid the avoidable pitfalls, and a structure on which you can build your own career success. Here's where the story of your life becomes important. Yes, you can benefit from hindsight too, if you study the learning of people who have been there before you. But how many of us take advantage of that?

## CAREER IS A STORY

If you ask someone about their career what you'll get is a fascinating tale of ups and downs over a period of time from school to the present day. They'll tell you their life story. And it is life because career and life interact in ways which impact on each other. For some people their career is their life and for others their life is their career. But one thing you'll notice is that people so often fail to learn from the lessons of the past, both in life and in career, largely because they're so busy living out their life story they've no time to reflect on what's gone before.

The problem is the story lives in the mind so it's not easy to see it as a whole. And the mind has a habit of distorting memories to suit present day thinking. A good way of overcoming this is to write down your story as it happens. Keep a diary, or a journal, or a learning log. That way you'll build up a record of your learning experiences. You'll create your own personal career story – much easier to look back on than a collection of scattered thoughts.

## WRITING AIDS THINKING

The interesting thing about writing is that it makes you think. How often when you want to write something do you sit looking at a blank sheet of paper, or a blank computer screen, nibbling the end of your pencil or playing with the mouse, and trying to decide what it is you want to say?

Then you start writing the first few words and ideas begin to flow. Writing and thinking, thinking and writing. Pretty soon you've done half a page and you look back to see how what you've written hangs together. You think about it and maybe you change something. Or what you've just read gives you another idea for the next paragraph.

Can you see the obvious benefit of applying this to your career? Very often it's not until we have to write about an experience that we really think about it. What went right and why? What went wrong and why? What did we learn from the experience? How might we do things differently next time? What did we learn about ourself? Do we have a knowledge gap? A development need? This process of reflection is a powerful learning tool.

Another thing I've found is that I frequently don't know exactly what I want to say in any detail about a topic until I've started writing about it. Searching for meaning in my thoughts and ideas as I write becomes a creative process that generates new ways of thinking, so writing things down can create insight that otherwise might be lost for ever.

So writing your own career story is about using reflection and insight to create your own hindsight. How useful is that?

## COMMITTING TO PAPER

Some people love writing and need no further motivation. Others find it a tiresome chore to be avoided at all costs, so they'll have to focus on self-motivation. If you belong to the second group, convince yourself that what you're doing is going to be helpful in developing your self-awareness, and that in turn is going to help you achieve your true potential. It's along the route to the job satisfaction and sense of life fulfilment you're seeking. So just do it.

But do tailor your writing to your feelings about writing. Those who enjoy it will find no difficulty in keeping a learning journal and probably already have some form of journal or diary. At the other end of the scale, especially if you aren't used to writing down your thoughts and feelings, start small with a simple learning log.

Just keep a record of any activity that gave you some kind of learning. Shakespeare puts it eloquently in the quotation at the head of this chapter, reminding us that learning is everywhere around us if we look for it. It could be reading a book, watching a DVD, attending a course of training or education, watching TV, talking to the postman, reading the morning paper, sitting watching the sun go down. In fact, anything. The important thing is to keep your mind constantly alert to the idea that insightful learning can come from the most unexpected directions.

Here's a simple example from my life in an old learning log entry of mine.

| Date | What I did | What I learned |
|---|---|---|
| 26 Jun 09 | Chatted to lifeguard at swimming pool and discovered he's a British Judo Team member | • Achievement in sport is similar to achievement in career<br><br>• Attitude is key to being a winner<br><br>• Need to read up on motivation in sport to see what I can learn about techniques that may be useful in career self-management |

And here's the story it's based on:

### A SESSION AT THE SWIMMING POOL

*Climbed out of the pool after a long swim and flopped into a lounger. Began chatting to the lifeguard and discovered he was a British judo champion. We talked about training for the Olympics and about top level competitive sporting standards.*

*I asked him: since fighters at that level are all the same weight, follow the same training and diet regimes, have similar fitness and experience, how could one overcome another and separate out into gold, silver, and bronze. His reply was simple. 'It's all down to attitude. All other things being equal the one with the stronger will to win will win, so we have a sports psychologist to help hone attitude.'*

*That got me thinking about career and personal development, and what a difference attitude makes. How attitude is linked to the self-confidence that comes from self-awareness and from the right kind of focused training and development. And how we can see that the people we judge to be successful in life are so often ordinary people with extraordinary attitude.*

*From there I felt encouraged to study some of the writing on sporting achievement which led me to ideas about mental imagery and visualization as tools to boost motivation.*

*I didn't expect to find that kind of learning when I struck up a casual poolside conversation, but it was there because my mind was open to any experience that might teach me something.*

In a learning log you need write only two or three short bullet points to remind yourself of what it was you learned from the situation. Stay excited about what you've learned, so don't feel you have to write more than you need to jog your memory when you look back. But if you do enjoy writing let it flow. The important thing is not how much you write but how much you've learned. Over the months and years ahead you'll build up a valuable dossier about yourself and your learning. Looking back over it you'll be amazed at how much you've progressed.

## LEARNING FROM ACTION LEARNING

If you've been able to set up or join an Action Learning group (see Chapter 7) you'll have an excellent structure to help with the recording of your learning. If you're working alone on your career use the following explanation for clues on how you might adapt it to develop your learning log.

The Learning Triangle, an idea developed by Professor David Botham and Professor John Morris at the Revans Institute for Action Learning and Research, helps us understand how we should record our learning. Here's what the Learning Triangle looks like:

Source: see Notes to Chapter 8

The M at the centre of the triangle stands for Monitoring, a reminder that if we want to get the most from our learning we have to monitor it. The way we monitor it is to write about it in our learning journal or learning log. The three sides of the triangle tell us what it is we should monitor.

> Work is the project, the issues, and the problems we bring to Action Learning. What we record are the lessons learned from involvement in the process of problem solving.
>
> Set reminds us to write about what we've learned from being part of an Action Learning set. For those working alone you could record what you've learned from interaction with others.
>
> Information is about the learning we pick up largely from activity outside the Action Learning set – for example, reading, training courses, lectures, films, casual conversations and so on.

In recording our learning it's important to remember to write about what we've learned about ourselves. These will be among the most important lessons we learn.

## THE ADDED VALUE OF KEEPING A LEARNING RECORD

The greatest value to you in keeping a learning journal or learning log will be in the process of reflection and insight while you're writing it. Reflection should include frequently looking back to recall old learning as it's all too easy to forget the lessons of the past, especially if they aren't part of your day to day work routine. Looking back over what you've written not only refreshes the memory but helps you create new learning as you begin to make links between entries. Maybe something you wrote last year makes more sense when you compare it with something you wrote last month, and this could lead you on to new insights.

But there are many other uses for the information you've gathered. For example you could use it:

> At appraisal and performance review time to make sure your line manager is fully briefed on your achievements and development over the period.
>
> To negotiate for promotion or pay review.
>
> To prepare yourself for assessment or development centres.
>
> To negotiate for a role change or an internal transfer.
>
> When looking for a new job.
>
> In putting your CV together.
>
> If thinking about a career change.
>
> When making decisions about education and training courses.
>
> To write an action plan for your development needs.

**NEXT CHAPTER**

In Chapter 9 we think about the idea of setting ourselves targets and goals. Setting objectives gives us a sense of purpose and direction in our career, so it's a crucial part of our personal development.

# CHAPTER 9

> *Large streams from little fountains flow,*
> *Tall oaks from little acorns grow.*
>
> David Everett, Lines written for a school
> declamation by a little boy of seven, 1797.

# SETTING LEARNING OBJECTIVES

## CAREER AND LIFE DIRECTION

A good map is a godsend in unfamiliar territory. It helps us pinpoint where we are and it shows the way to our chosen destination. So we can navigate with confidence. But what use is the map if we don't know where we're going?

Career self-management is very much like that. We've invested time in developing the MAP, or motivation, ability, personality of self-identity (Chapter 4), and in learning the art of career navigation (Chapter 6). Chapter 5 offered the skills needed for successful career self-management, and Chapter 8 showed how to record and reflect on learning. But in moving forward it's useful to have some idea of both the ultimate goal and the waymarkers along the route.

Waymarkers are more than just a guide to achievement. As we see from the Treasure Chest on Stress Management, a sense of career and life direction breeds aspiration, gives hope, and offers the means by which it's possible to find job satisfaction and fulfilment in life. So they become tools in confidence building, in searching for a satisfying future, and in seeking to develop a stress tolerant lifestyle.

In career and life development our waymarkers are the outcomes of tasks and goals we set ourselves in striving to reach a destination. They might begin with an evening class, lead on to a formal qualification, and end with a new career. Or the plan could be to learn to drive, to become more independent, and to gain in self-confidence from doing that. For each stage of such journeys setting targets, or objectives, will help us monitor progress and give us a goal to aim for. But let's stop for a moment and consider the meaning behind some of these ideas.

## IDEALS AND REALITY

### *Moving Targets*

I've talked here about destinations and ultimate goals, but one thing it's important to understand is that throughout life destinations can change and the ultimate goal keeps on moving ahead. This is not a problem: in fact it's an exciting and energizing process. Let me explain.

Most people have much more potential than they believe they have, but it's not easy to know this without the right kind of experience or without some good quality career guidance. As you begin to develop your potential, sometimes by chance, sometimes through a career plan, you start to become aware that there's more you could achieve. Achievement could be practical through work roles or it could be through academic qualifications. Whichever, you get the feeling you could go onward and upward.

So your destination changes from a lower level to a higher level. And what seemed like an ultimate goal a few years back now looks like an intermediate step on the way to something better. The thought of achieving that goal, and then an even more challenging goal, begins to form. And so it goes on for as long as you have the courage and the determination to make it happen. The point is you never reach your ultimate because the imagined ultimate becomes your ideal. How could anyone ever reach that point of perfection beyond which no further development is possible?

## *The Vision Of Ideals And The Rocks Of Reality*

So is it worth having ideals? Is it worth aspiring to something we feel is beyond our lifetime reach? Is it worth daring to hope we can achieve a dream? Yes! Yes! Yes! For one thing, because we all have unused potential we can never be sure we can't achieve something greater than we have at present. We don't know until we try. For another, as I've already explained, each level of achievement opens up new and greater opportunities that enable us to push our ideal further on. It's only looking back you realize how far you've come, and by how much you've exceeded your initial expectations.

Of course the road won't always be smooth and straight. There'll be hills to climb and rocky paths to slow you down. But your ideal is your beacon. It's the vision of a goal towards which you strive despite the problems along the way. At times it may be tempting to compromise your ideal and to settle for something less when moving ahead seems impossible. This is the testing time of the true Career Warrior. To compromise is to settle for less than your true worth. To battle on is the way to achievement of your true potential. The world has seen many ordinary people achieve extraordinary things by maintaining the strength of their ideal in times of trouble. Why shouldn't you be one of them?

## **WRITING OBJECTIVES**

The achievement of goals is helped by setting objectives along the way, waymarkers as I called them earlier. It's the equivalent of looking at the map, deciding where it is we want to go, and planning the route to get there. And in career management, just as in any journey, it's possible to have both a long-term destination and shorter-term stopping off points. These are our objectives. We always write them down, and we keep them in a place where we see them frequently. If you've taken the advice of Chapter 8 on keeping a learning journal you'll have the best place to keep your objectives – right at the front of your journal.

We write down objectives for two good reasons. First, as Chapter 8 explains, the process of writing things down, makes you think hard about what it is you want to say. So your objectives will be clear and well thought through. Second, when we commit things to writing we are more likely to take action on them.

It's important in objective setting to be realistic. Set targets and goals that are achievable given your circumstances and resources. Setting goals too high can be demotivating and bring anxiety when we find ourselves unable to achieve them, so don't be afraid of starting small. Our chapter quotation reminds us that small beginnings can lead to big outcomes, and that it takes time to get there – but don't think you can't start out with an ideal. It's just that you have to fit your dream into reality.

## General Rules Of Objective Setting

Objective setting has become standard procedure in many organizations, and it's the practice to follow the acronym SMART in writing down objectives.

### THE MEANING OF SMART

*Specific:* Objectives should be clear about what exactly is to be achieved (e.g. NVQ Level 3 in Health and Social Care).

*Measurable:* Objectives should have a clear outcome that can be assessed against some standard (e.g. attainment of NVQ Level 3).

*Achievable:* What you are aiming for should be a realistic goal in line with your previous qualifications and experience and within your resources of time and money.

*Relevant:* Your objectives should be linked to where it is you want to be in your career or your life.

*Timed:* Your objectives should include a deadline for achieving your goal.

SMART is a useful framework for writing objectives, but it's important not to set targets too high too soon. Failure to achieve objectives is pretty demotivating. On the other hand success is encouraging. So do make your objectives realistic and give yourself a chance, especially if this is new territory for you. Yes objectives should be challenging, but they shouldn't be so tough it's impossible to fulfil them.

## *Sharing Is A Powerful Learning Tool*

It's really helpful to show your objectives to someone who will ask you questions about them and challenge your thinking. If you are part of an Action Learning set (Chapter 7) this will be the ideal place to discuss your ideas. If you are working alone on your development try to think of someone you feel can be trusted with your special thoughts and ideas. Someone who will take your objectives seriously and encourage you in them, but who will also ask you the important 'why' questions.

If that person is also able and willing to support you by taking an interest in your progress as you work through your objectives this would be a great bonus. You might in turn be able to help them by sharing what you've learned from this book.

## *The World Keeps On Turning*

Having set your objectives it's vital to monitor them closely over time. The world around us is constantly changing, and so are we. Law, government rules and regulations, the education system, management practice are frequently reviewed and changed or updated. And as we grow and mature as people our values, interests, and beliefs change too.

So however carefully you design your objectives they may need to be changed from time to time to reflect the changing world. It's good practice to check your objectives frequently, and if you keep them in a place where you see them often they'll be easy to check. I've suggested the front of your learning journal as a good place to keep objectives. You might also put a copy on your desk at work, or in the corner of your home you use for your personal thinking.

### Short And Long-Term Objectives

It's a good idea to have both short-term and longer-term objectives. If you have a really good sense of career direction you might have medium-term objectives too.

Short-term might be a month ahead, longer-term maybe the next six months to a year. With a well developed career plan you might have short-term objectives for three months, medium-term for a year, and long-term three years. But really there are no rules about this. It's very much up to you and will depend on the level of commitment you want to give, or are able to give, to your development.

### Examples Of Objectives

If you're already skilled at objective writing you'll not need further advice. If you do need some help look at the examples in the Treasure Chest in Part 4.

### A Life Mission Statement

When you feel you've mastered the skills of the Career Warrior your long-term objective, if you feel sufficiently passionate about it, can become a lifetime objective. A lifetime objective is something not everybody will want to commit to or be able to achieve. This will come only after a prolonged period of personal development and a great deal of reflection on self-identity. And only if you want it. Don't look for this too early in life, and don't feel you need to have a lifetime objective if it doesn't fit with your lifestyle. But don't be afraid of it either. A lifetime objective is about reaching out for the ultimate goal of achieving your true potential. It's about having a career or life ideal.

Writing a lifetime objective is a bit like writing a mission statement for an organization. It's a statement of your mission in life. A commitment to an ideal you'll have developed over some years. The easiest way to illustrate this is to offer my own life mission statement as an example.

## LIFE MISSION STATEMENT

*My life mission is to help people discover their true potential, and to assist them in finding ways of achieving it.*

To make such a commitment is both scary and liberating. It's scary because you realize it's a lifetime commitment and it may cause difficulties in other parts of your life. But it's liberating because in terms of career navigation (Chapter 6) you take personal control of your life and steer your career and your life into alignment with your personal characteristics of motivation, ability, and personality. A well thought through life mission statement will give you a highly developed sense of career and life direction and purpose, thus creating the right kind of conditions for job satisfaction and a sense of fulfilment in life.

The interesting thing about this stage of your career is that objectives are no longer written in terms of a specific career field. With my life mission statement I don't have to choose between career roles such as teacher, trainer, psychologist, consultant, or anything else. I simply find things to do that match my life mission, whatever they are. I could be working one to one on career coaching, or I could be running a team building exercise for a business team, or it could be coaching a manager experiencing workplace stress, or setting up Action Learning for a group of voluntary sector workers. Self-employment gives great flexibility for doing this.

Or I could take a job in personnel management, or in career coaching within an organization so long as I could keep a reasonable amount of control over navigating my career in the direction I want it to go. I've done this too.

Can you see what has happened here? Traditionally we look at careers and try to identify a field of work that suits us. With a life mission we decide who we are, what we want to do with our lives, and then go out and find ways of doing it. We've turned the whole business around so that we control the direction of our lives instead of allowing our lives to be driven by what our limited vision of working life tells us is available. I call this looking through the other end of the telescope.

**NEXT CHAPTER**

It's always useful to see what we might learn from the experience of those who've gone before us. Chapter 10 gives us that opportunity with illustrations from the learning journals of Career Warriors I've worked with.

Read this chapter to get a feeling for what is possible. Or read it when you feel a need for a boost in your motivation.

***So what is possible for you?***

# CHAPTER 10

> *He that stays in the valley shall never get over the hill.*
>
> John Ray, *Catalogue of English Proverbs,* 1670.

## LEARNING FROM EXAMPLE – WHAT CAREER WARRIORS SAY

### THE NAMING OF THE WARRIORS

As part of my research work in 1999 and 2000 I ran three Career Warrior programmes, all as Action Learning groups, and asked participants if I could read and analyze their personal learning journals. Reading their journals over and over again as part of the process of analysis I was frequently deeply moved by the frankness of their personal disclosures and the joy of their self-discovery.

I feel very protective of the trust those Career Warriors have given me in sharing their thoughts and feelings with me, and to safeguard the confidentiality of their private stories I promised the people involved I would not use their real names in anything I wrote. Instead, I hit on the idea of giving them the names of characters taken from Sir Thomas Malory's legendary tales of King Arthur. So if the names of our Career Warriors sound a little familiar you now know why.

### THE WORDS OF THE WARRIORS

These extracts from personal learning journals can give only an idea of how the Career Warrior programme impacted on the lives of those participating in it. All those involved worked at their development over a period of nine to twelve months, beginning in their personal valley and aiming for the hill they saw in front of them. When our programme ended some had reached the peak of their hill; some were still climbing but could see the way ahead to their summit.

## What can you learn from their experience?

Lyonesse

**After a few months**: 'I am learning constantly about myself from others.'

Alice

**After a year**: 'In the last year, due to Career Warrior, I have concentrated on more detail of my skill development than I think I ever have. This has helped me stop and think about the way other people may see me.'

Gareth

**First session**: 'I need to be back in control, build self-esteem, get back sense of worth and hope and enthusiasm.'

**One year later**: 'I have changed from giving up completely to gaining self-worth, recognition, and helping others, but also getting a degree of self-control back.'

Lisle

**After three months**: 'Feelings on Career Warrior to date. It's getting more complex and messy – no immediate answers yet but feeling more in control. Am unravelling my situation properly for the first time – am feeling confident about sorting it out.'

**After five months**: 'On a real journey. Real because it's at my pace and because I'm being pushed to deal with and get to the core of the real problem. There's good support and challenge, and the group is confidential and non judgemental.'

**After nine months**: 'I feel like a new person. My job is on a roll in all directions.'

Anglides

**First session**: 'Career Warrior makes sense. I like the idea of acquiring armour, weapons, wiles as you proceed through life – it corresponds with acquiring social attributes and skills.'

**After four months**: 'Through the support of colleagues times of difficulty and distress are confronted and overcome – true of our group. I find the others very supportive. I value the questioning and prodding. I need this.'

Baudwin

**After a year**: 'Decisions which I would have agonized over a year ago I now make without noticing. Phone calls which I would have put off for several days I now just make. I run up the hills and I am becoming confident enough to start tackling the mountains.'

Elaine

**After eight months**: 'When I examine my objectives for the programme I find I do have a clearer idea of career direction. I have taken control of my personal development rather than leave it to others. I feel also that I have a much stronger sense of my own strengths and weaknesses.'

Guinevere

**After eight months**: 'Listening to other members of the group and their problems has reinforced the thought that whatever industry we work in, and whoever we are, our problems are more or less the same.'

Elizabeth

**After a year**: 'There are three strands to my self-discovery through the Career Warrior programme. First I learnt that my intellectual abilities are far greater than I had imagined. Secondly, I came to terms with the true extent to which I am value driven. Thirdly, I realized that the only limiting factors are my self-confidence and my ability to stay focused. These discoveries have done much for my self-confidence. I have realized over the past few months that I have much more to offer than I have given myself credit for.'

Tristram

**After a year**: 'Some groundwork has already been started towards the achievement of my medium-term objective. This is where I feel that the experience and insight gained through participating in the Career Warrior programme will be of benefit to me in the future although it may not be immediately apparent as to how this will be achieved. They say that everything comes to he who waits – Career Warrior can hopefully cut down the waiting period.'

*Lynet*

**After nine months**: 'I am clearer about what I want, how to get it, how I learn, how I don't learn, what improvements I need to make and how to go about making those improvements.'

*Lioners*

**February**: 'I am going to make a real effort with the main area for improvement which is my confidence and once this has increased I will find everything easier to tackle.'

**March**: 'I am getting braver and more confident all the time.'

**November**: 'My confidence in general has soared.'

## AND A WORD FROM A LINE MANAGER

One of the Career Warrior groups was a business team who completed the programme together. I discouraged their line manager, let's call him Merlin, from joining the programme because I thought his presence might prevent the team being totally open and honest. At the end of the programme I asked Merlin for his comments on whether he felt his team had benefited from Career Warrior. Here's what he wrote.

> 'Is the idea of encouraging employees to become Career Warriors useful to organizations? In our experience the answer is a resounding YES. We have seen these individuals grow in stature, we have seen a dynamic team move to new dimensions, including inducting to the team a new member and transferring this 'buzz' to them.
>
> I can see how it could be a fear of some organizations that you give these individuals new skills, the ability to manage their own career and personal development, and before you know it they move on. Our experience is totally the reverse.
>
> These people fully revelled in taking control of their own development, they loved finding out so much about themselves and debating issues and problems with their colleagues in the Action Learning sets of Career Warrior (something they still do). But above all they joined in the satisfaction that their improved performance is benefiting the most important thing – their customers.'

Of course it says much for Merlin that he created the right environment in which his team could flourish.

## NEXT CHAPTER
Well this is the last chapter from me. The next chapter is up to you.

***Where do you want to take it from here?***

# PART 4

## The Treasure Chest

A box full of career and life mangement skills

# OPEN THE BOX

| | |
|---|---|
| Getting professional career guidance | 103 |
| The MAP Exercise: getting at your motivation, ability, and personality | 108 |
| The Career Warrior's weapons: skills for career self-management | 113 |
| Checking the quality of match: you – your job – the job you want | 142 |
| *Super Trouper*: spotlight on Action Learning | 146 |
| Examples of career objectives | 152 |
| A framework for organizational good practice in career self-management | 157 |

# GETTING PROFESSIONAL CAREER GUIDANCE

## (REFER TO CHAPTER 4)

# GETTING PROFESSIONAL CAREER GUIDANCE

*YOU CAN GET IT FREE*

*Free careers information, advice, and guidance is available to people of all ages living in the UK via one of three websites. Contacts are:*

*England and Northern Ireland: nationalcareersservice.direct.gov.uk or telephone 0800 100 900.*

*Scotland: www.myworldofwork.co.uk or telephone 0808 100 1050.*

*Wales: www.careerswales.com or telephone 0800 100 900.*

*On offer from these excellent sites is free advice by email, phone, and webchat with face to face help available at a local centre near you. The website has a range of easy to use online career tools including skills and interests checking, CV builder, action planner, funding advice, space for your learning record, and much more.*

*What is not on offer is the more in-depth psychological profiling, including the use of psychometric tests, normally provided by specialist practitioners. You'll have to pay for this kind of service (see next page on how to find a private practitioner).*

*I strongly recommend anyone seeking help with their career to begin by accessing these sites. Even if you've decided to pay a private provider for a more in-depth personal service your career thinking will benefit greatly from first working through your national careers service.*

*For English speaking people living outside the UK I suggest you make use of these excellent websites. You'll not be able to access the personal support available to UK residents but you will find the various tools and advice very useful in your career thinking and planning.*

## IF YOU CHOOSE TO PAY

*You're about to make an investment in your future so you owe it to yourself to find the best possible guidance you can afford. This doesn't mean best is the most expensive, but it does mean looking around to find the best person for you.*

*In the UK, if you want the assurance of a trained and qualified career coach backed by a professional body, a good place to start is the British Psychological Society (www.bps.org.uk). On their website you'll find the directory of chartered psychologists, and listed under Vocational Assessment and Career Issues are the names and contact details of psychologists offering career services.*

*If you don't own a computer you'll probably find free access to one at your local library, and if you have trouble navigating your way through the directory don't be shy about asking a librarian for help. That's what librarians do. They help people find information. And good librarians love doing that.*

*The benefit of using a chartered psychologist is that registration with the British Psychological Society requires set standards of qualifications and experience. Chartered psychologists are also bound by a professional code of conduct (printed at the end of their online directory) and subject to disciplinary action if they behave unprofessionally. So you can have confidence that your interests are protected.*

*Many psychologists are also registered as state regulated practitioners. This means their professional titles are genuine and they meet national standards of competence. You can check their status on the Health Professions Council website (www.hpc-uk.org).*

*It's not essential to be a psychologist to be a good career coach. For example, the Institute of Career Guidance (www.icg-uk.org) has a register of independent guidance practitioners, and advanced practitioners, who meet the Institute's standards of qualification and who commit to ethical practice.*

*If you do have difficulty finding a career coach near where you live, contact your national careers service. They should be able to help you.*

## CHECKING OUT YOUR CAREER COACH

*My advice is to contact three career coaches and discuss your requirements with all of them. Ideally this initial discussion should be face to face, but you can do it on the telephone if a meeting isn't possible. This exploratory session should be free and with no strings attached.*

*Choose to work with the one you feel most comfortable with, but it's courteous to let the others know your decision. Reputable career coaches will have no problem with this. They will understand and respect your decision.*

*Run a mile from anyone who offers to solve all your problems and promises to find you your perfect career match. Nobody can do this for you. The career coach's job is to help you understand yourself better, to help you explore options, and to challenge your thinking – in short, to help you help yourself.*

*Don't hesitate to ask coaches about their qualifications, their experience, and the way they work. A good coach will expect this.*

*Always ask these questions before you enter into any agreement:*

> *How much does the service cost?*
>
> *Does that include VAT?*
>
> *What exactly will I get for my money?*
>
> *For what period of time does the service run?*
>
> *If I need further help is there a cost, and if so how much?*
>
> *Could I speak to someone you've worked with?*

*Before you accept any agreement insist on having a written description of the service and the costs. Good coaches will welcome these questions because they will want you to feel comfortable and confident about working with them.*

## PSYCHOMETRIC TESTING

*Coaches often use tests and questionnaires to gather information on motivation, aptitude, and personality, although some coaches prefer not to use them. These psychometric tests, as they're called, can be paper and pencil or computer managed. There's no hard and fast rule about it. What is important is what's right for you. I like psychometric tests because they help me make sense of the coaching process. I find the people who come to me for career analysis and guidance like them too because they provide a structure that helps them understand and retain information about themselves.*

*If offered psychometric testing, ask the coach to confirm that she or he is qualified to administer and interpret such tests. UK coaches qualified in testing will have trained with, and been awarded certification by, one or more of the many test publishers. It's not necessary to be a psychologist to be qualified in psychometric testing for career assessment.*

*Check counsellors' test qualifications against their names on the BPS Register of Qualifications in Test Use (www.psychtesting.org.uk) where you will also find a great deal of information and advice on test taking, including links to publishers who offer practice tests. If your coach is not registered you can check their test qualifications with the publishers of the tests they intend to use with you.*

*Ask coaches for information about the tests they intend to use and, for aptitude testing, ask for sample tests to practise on in advance of your career assessment day.*

*Warning*

*Psychometric tests are only part of the process of career analysis and guidance. They should be used in conjunction with one to one career coaching, and test results should always be discussed in depth with you.*

*No test can describe you with total accuracy, so if the results don't feel right always query them with your coach. A good career coach will expect you to do this and will welcome the opportunity to answer your questions.*

# THE MAP EXERCISE

## GETTING AT YOUR MOTIVATION ABILITY AND PERSONALITY

## (REFER TO CHAPTER 4)

# THE MAP EXERCISE

## GETTING AT YOUR MOTIVATION ABILITY AND PERSONALITY

Take some time out in a quiet place and write down your thoughts in the boxes that follow these notes.

Under Motivation jot down those aspects of work that bring you enjoyment, job satisfaction, and a sense of pride in achievement. The things about work that you really like and look forward to. Is it working on a PC? Is it totting up rows and columns of figures? Is it about giving a service to people? Working on your own or working as part of a team? Are you happier working at a desk in an office or do you prefer to be up and about, maybe outdoors?

Under Ability, list your knowledge and skills. Include qualifications from school, college, university, evening classes, adult education. What training courses have you done, and what on-job learning experience do you have? What other skills have you gained from sport, hobbies, travel? It'll be difficult for you to know about your aptitude because this requires formal testing, but you may have a feel for where your strongest talents lie. Are you greatly better with words than with figures, or vice versa? Do you have a talent for drawing, painting, music, sport, craft, mechanical things?

Under Personality, try to assess the way you are with people and situations. Do you like to spend your time working with people or working alone? Do you enjoy taking the lead in things? Which feels best, organizing and managing other people or getting on with the job yourself? Would you rather work with people or with tools and machines? Are you happiest in a team or better at one to one and small group situations? What feels best, working where facts are the most important thing or working where feelings and emotions come more into play? How much freedom to do your own thing do you want?

You may have some difficulty with this exercise because it's very hard to make honest judgements about yourself. Show your list to someone whose opinion you trust and value and ask them if this sounds like you. Remember you may not get totally honest feedback as people may be afraid of hurting your feelings. Better still, find another person who is interested in doing the same exercise – then you can swap notes on each other agreeing to be as honest as you can without giving or taking offence.

*TO FIND THE ANSWERS TO THE **ME** SHEETS*
*(see next page)*

*Give some deep thought to it.*

*Ask your friends and relatives.*

*Think back through all your education, training courses, and on-job learning to remember the skills you've acquired.*

*Think carefully about your activities outside work, your hobbies, your sport. What knowledge and skills have you developed there that you could use in your career role?*

*What are your life values? What do you feel passionate about?*

*What was your dream career at school, college, or university? Is it still relevant?*

*Do you feel you've missed your true vocation? What was it? Is it still relevant?*

```
              /\
             /  \
            /    \
 MOTIVATION/      \ABILITY
          /        \
         / SELF-IDENTITY \
        /            \
       /_____\
          PERSONALITY
```

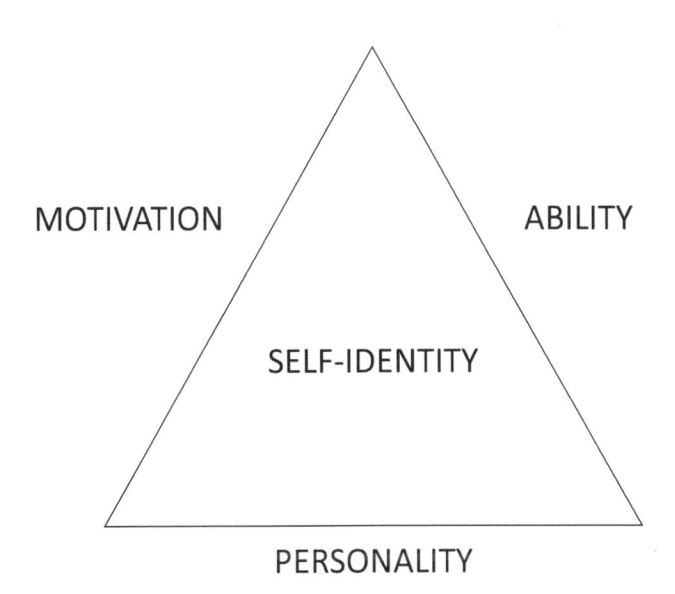

ME: ⟶
      ⬇

> *MOTIVATION (What I enjoy doing; what gives me a sense of pride and satisfaction in my work).*
>
>
>
>
>
>
>
>
>
> *Example:  I love working with people, helping them and giving them advice and guidance.*

*ABILITY   (My knowledge, skills, and experience).*

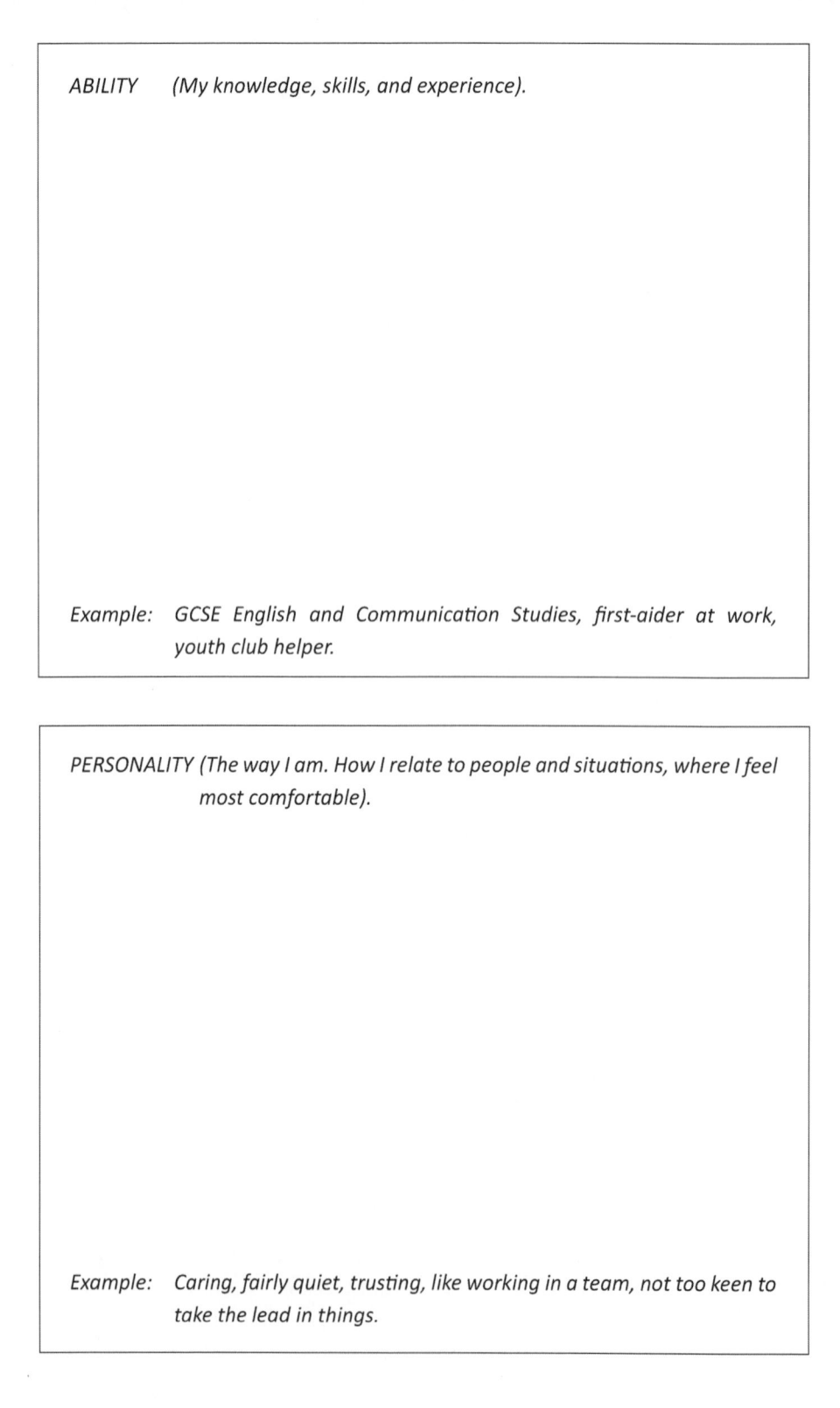

*Example:   GCSE English and Communication Studies, first-aider at work, youth club helper.*

*PERSONALITY (The way I am. How I relate to people and situations, where I feel most comfortable).*

*Example:   Caring, fairly quiet, trusting, like working in a team, not too keen to take the lead in things.*

# THE CAREER WARRIOR'S WEAPONS

## SKILLS FOR CAREER SELF-MANAGEMENT

## (REFER TO CHAPTER 5)

NOTE: These skills sheets are written as notes because each area is the subject of considerable research and writing which you can follow up if you need to. There's sufficient information in each sheet to give you the core understanding you need to begin to use the skill.

| | |
|---|---|
| Self-Marketing | 115 |
| Networking | 118 |
| Organizational Politics | 120 |
| Interpersonal Skills | 123 |
| Proactivity | 126 |
| Creating Opportunities | 129 |
| Leadership | 132 |
| Stress Management | 135 |
| Action Learning | 141 |

# SELF-MARKETING

> *The ability and the confidence to sell oneself, not in an overbearing and pompous way, but appropriately and based on the insight of self-awareness. Keeping an excellent up to date CV and acquiring good interview skills are important components.*

## INTRODUCTION

This is a vital skill for Career Warriors because it's important in career development. Some people are naturally good at promoting themselves, some believe that 'blowing your own trumpet' is bad behaviour. How you feel about self-marketing often depends on where you were brought up and how you were taught to behave.

So is it good or bad to self-market? Well that depends on how you do it. Do it responsibly, do it appropriately, and don't lie. There's nothing wrong with being proud of your abilities and achievements, and telling the right people about them. If you don't your special talents may remain hidden and this does nobody any good.

## SELF AS PRODUCT

Ask someone to sell their company's products or ideas and they have no problem. Ask them to sell themselves and they suddenly see that as tacky. But this isn't true if you market yourself appropriately. Whether you're looking for promotion, for a new job, or just to get your ideas across you're a product and you need to be marketed effectively. So do your product research and launch your self-marketing public relations campaign. There are many ways of keeping your image alive and letting the world know what you're capable of.

| | |
|---|---|
| In Writing | CV – letters – memos – reports – minutes of meetings – email – social networks – business plans – suggestion schemes – appraisals – company newsletter – professional journals – PR/media opportunities. |
| In Speech | Interviews – appraisals – meetings – committees – briefings – social functions – networking – telephone – coaching – training – talking in the corridor. |
| Appearance and Manner | Clothes – grooming – example – attitude – caring – concern for others – recognition of others. |
| Be Assertive | Learn the skills and boost your confidence in self-marketing. |

*ASSERTIVENESS*
*(find the middle way)*

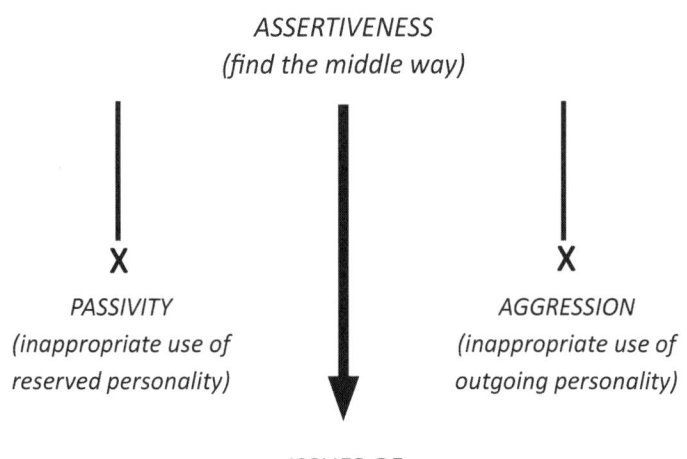

| | | |
|---|---|---|
| X | ↓ | X |
| *PASSIVITY* | | *AGGRESSION* |
| *(inappropriate use of reserved personality)* | | *(inappropriate use of outgoing personality)* |

*ISSUES OF SELF-CONFIDENCE*

*WHAT MIGHT AFFECT SELF-CONFIDENCE*

*Early development*  
*School*  
*Socialization*

*Traumatic event*  
*(e.g. bereavement,*  
*divorce, redundancy)*

*ACTIVITIES FOR LOW SELF-CONFIDENCE*

*Build confidence and self-esteem by improving skills and knowledge.*

*With bad experiences think about how you could have managed things better, write down what you learned, and use that learning next time.*

*Practise in a safe environment first.*

*Don't take on too much too soon.*

*Go for some quick wins to reinforce learning.*

*Understand people and communicate appropriately.*

*Stick to your views when you know you're right.*

*Books, DVDs, audio tapes, courses on assertiveness skills.*

# NETWORKING

> *Making and maintaining contact with people inside and outside the organization who can help overcome problems through the sharing of information and ideas.*

## INTRODUCTION

What makes a network? Think Interpol. Think transport systems. Think the body's central nervous system. They are all there for a similar purpose – to enable the smooth travel of people and information through an organized system. And so it is with groups of people who support each other through exchanges of information.

We need networks to help us exchange knowledge, ideas, and learning. They could be formal, for example a trade union or professional association related to your career role. They could be informal such as an old school club, a chat site on the internet, or a local business club. Or you could just start up your own by keeping a list of the names and contact details of people you meet in your day to day work. Or by using social networks like LinkedIn, Twitter, and Facebook. The point is the same. Knowing where to turn to for help in solving problems, and returning the favour when someone else in your network needs assistance.

## VALUE OF NETWORKS

Exchange of information – mutual help – support – different ways of looking at things – introductions – staying at the forefront of knowledge – opportunity spotting – self-marketing – selling – avoiding disaster areas – awareness of people – initiating joint ventures – avenue for giving.

## ESTABLISHING A NETWORK CONTACT

Consider best medium of approach: telephone call or email for routine knowledge sharing or social networks – formal letter if approaching senior managers – but tailor approach to situation and to person being approached.

Don't ask network contacts for jobs, ask for a chat to discuss career opportunities and current market situations.

## JOINING FORMAL NETWORKS

Look for opportunities to join networks that will be useful to you in your career. For example, Management Development Network – Continuing Personal Development Network – local women's or men's network – professional groups (e.g. Chartered Management Institute, Association for Project Management) – Chamber of Commerce – business clubs – charities and voluntary groups.

## NETWORKING TIPS

Find out who's doing what – talk to people – swap business cards – write a few words about the person on the back of their card – offer help.

At network meetings latch onto someone you know to help you get started – wear a big name badge – prepare by deciding what kind of information you want – have a target for how many people you will meet – look for a list of who's there.

How about starting up your own network – at work (any topic you think might be useful to the organization) – from home (e.g. childcare group, craft enterprise, community support group).

# ORGANIZATIONAL POLITICS

> *Knowing what's going on around you, who's moving up and who's on a down. The wisdom to know when it's safe to speak your mind and when it's safer to keep your mouth firmly shut. Who and what brings success in the place you work.*

## GET IT IN PERSPECTIVE

People often say organizational politics is tacky and they won't put their nose in the trough. This is a wrong view. Just because some people have low morals it doesn't mean you have to be the same. Look on it as sensible intelligence gathering to help you manage your career appropriately. Understand the system and work from the inside.

## WHAT IT IS AND WHERE IT COMES FROM

Understanding the hidden tensions and power struggles within organizations. Awareness of the location of power and influence within the organization.

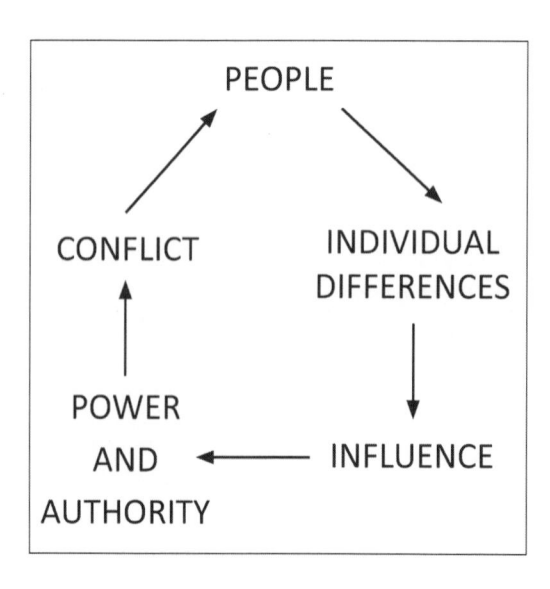

```
              PEOPLE
             ↗      ↘
      CONFLICT    INDIVIDUAL
         ↑        DIFFERENCES
                      ↓
      POWER
      AND  ←——— INFLUENCE
      AUTHORITY
```

People are different. That's life. So they have different ideas about how they should go about influencing events and activities around them. Different ways of doing things often generates power struggles, and power struggles lead to conflict. Conflict affects people, usually in a negative way, but it can be positive if used appropriately. That's why it's important to learn to manage organizational politics wisely.

## GOOD OR BAD?

Official influence comes via the management chain, so although it's not always liked it's understood as the official line of communication.

Sometimes people who aren't in a position of authority, or people who have a position of authority but wish to manipulate events in a direction different to the official line, work at influencing things in their own direction.

This kind of influence can be beneficial: e.g. union activity to prevent exploitation, bottom-up training initiatives, the prevention of injustice, exposure of fraud, whistle blowing, lobbying for more ethical practice, pushing for innovation. But it can also be a bad influence: e.g. getting rid of people whose face doesn't fit, solving personality clashes, personal gain.

## SHADOW COMMUNICATION

Non-official influence is conducted outside the normal channels of communication – the shadow side of the organization. This leads to 'grapevine communication', and to rumour, misinformation, disorder, confusion, error, and anxiety.

Political influence is usually about individuals' personal desires, goals, values, needs, aspirations. Thus we get power struggles and conflict.

## DRAWING YOUR LINE IN THE SAND

When you find it necessary to engage in organizational politics be cautious about whose lead you follow, how public you allow your support to be, and how much compromise you'll tolerate without sacrificing your principles. In making compromises keep tight hold on your true self-identity and use that knowledge to navigate yourself clear of career damage. Know when you reach the point beyond which you're not prepared to go and don't go there.

## IF IT'S REALLY NOT FOR YOU

Anyone aspiring to the highest levels of organizational life is unlikely to get there without some involvement in office politics. But if it does become impossible to handle don't waste time and energy cursing those who use this weapon. Instead, reassess the direction and purpose of your career quest, choose a different route where organizational politics is not an issue, and learn to live in harmony with your decision.

# INTERPERSONAL SKILLS

*The skill and the art of respecting and valuing people, of listening to others, of being approachable.*

## WHAT SKILL?

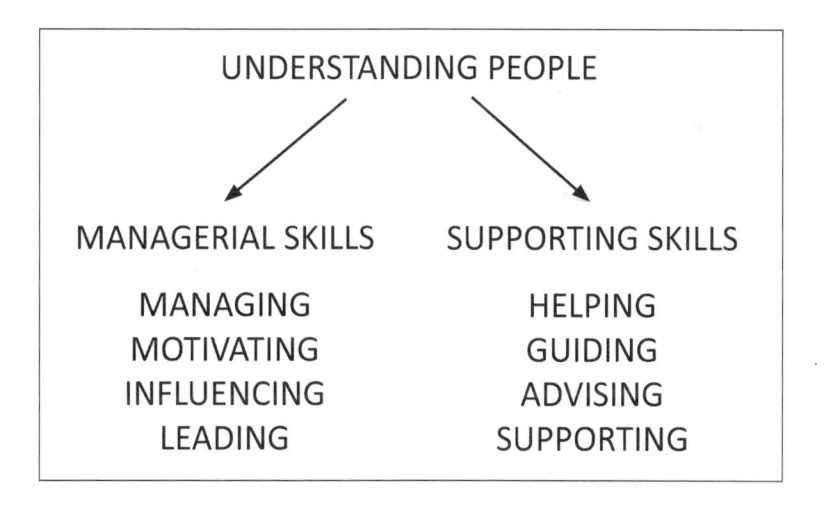

```
                UNDERSTANDING PEOPLE
                 ↙              ↘
    MANAGERIAL SKILLS      SUPPORTING SKILLS

         MANAGING                HELPING
        MOTIVATING               GUIDING
       INFLUENCING               ADVISING
         LEADING                SUPPORTING
```

## WHAT ART?

Sensitivity in the way in which you behave towards and communicate with people. Awareness and understanding of yourself as seen by the people you wish to influence so you can avoid alienating them. Awareness and understanding of the personal characteristics of others so you can communicate with them effectively.

## UNDERSTANDING

If you want to understand others you must first learn how to understand yourself.

Remember the armour of the Career Warrior – motivation, ability, personality (MAP). Use that as a tool to aid understanding of self and others, then communicate with people according to their MAP, in their style, in language that makes sense to them.

**PERSONAL SAFEGUARDS**

Work actively at developing the right characteristics for gaining trust and respect.

Don't lose your unique personal identity in adjusting your behaviour and communication style as a means of influencing others.

Know your limitations and don't be tempted to work beyond them.

**DEVELOPING A PERSONA**

Live your day to day life in such a way that you become the kind of person people trust and respect.

---

CHARACTERISTICS TO DEVELOP

| | |
|:---:|:---:|
| Listening skills | Confidentiality |
| Approachableness | Loyalty |
| Warmth | Trust |
| Empathy | Recognition of others |

Use appropriate body language

(eye contact, alertness, focus, position)

---

## ADVANCED APPLICATIONS OF INTERPERSONAL SKILLS

- Leading
- Managing
- Coaching
- Mentoring
- Counselling

## ACQUIRING SKILLS AND KNOWLEDGE

Library or Learning Centre for books, DVDs, audio tapes.

Internet sites offering high quality free learning (e.g. Open University, iTunes U), and free business and management facts sheets and research reports (e.g. Chartered Institute of Personnel and Development, Institute of Leadership and Management, The Charity Commission).

Courses at Regional Colleges, Colleges for Adult Education, University extra mural departments.

Observe people you respect and trust, seek their advice and support.

Consciously practise the use of interpersonal skills. Experiment first in a 'safe' environment, e.g. with relatives and friends before people at work; in social and recreational situations before more formal situations.

# PROACTIVITY

> *Not waiting for things to happen. Looking constantly for opportunities then figuring out how to exploit them. Delivering solutions rather than problems.*

## WHAT WE MEAN BY IT

The idea of proactivity has come into use to indicate the opposite of reactivity when talking about career and management development in organizations.

Whereas the reactive person waits for things to happen and then reacts to events, the proactive person constantly seeks to spot potential problems and opportunities and to do something positive about them. That way the proactive person stays ahead of the game, prevents problems occurring or at least limits the damage, and makes best use of opportunities for personal development.

## WHAT'S THE POINT?

In career self-management, being proactive is about creating opportunities instead of waiting for someone else to notice you or to give you a break. If you create your own opportunities you have more choice about your career direction. Using the armour of self-awareness as your guide you can navigate your career in line with your personal characteristics of motivation, ability, and personality.

## WHERE TO START

Self-awareness is the guiding force because it will stop you heading into areas that are wrong for you. Then getting to know what is going on in your organization, in the market you operate in, and in your profession becomes the learning priority. If you have a company intranet use it to keep up with what's going on in the organization. Read books, newspaper and journal articles, and staff correspondence related to your ideas – and network, network, network! Consider working for an academic or professional qualification. Before long you'll become expert in your field.

## CRITICAL SKILLS

In being proactive all the armour, weapons, and wiles of the Career Warrior must be employed. Self-awareness is crucial to knowing your strengths and limitations. Good networking skills and an understanding of organizational politics are needed to become aware of what is going on in your own and other organizations so you can create opportunities and counteract threats. Being proactive means selling your ideas, so good interpersonal skills and self-marketing become vital. It may also be necessary to take a leadership role, at least within the area you are seeking to exploit. Because being proactive usually involves doing something that isn't yet part of established practice, your workload is likely to increase, and others may be critical, so development of good stress tolerance is important. And pulling it all together in a way that benefits your career requires the skill of career navigation.

## EXPLOITING YOUR IDEAS

The point of being proactive is career development, so it's important to market your ideas.

This can be done in a number of ways:

> Keep your line manager informed and remind her/him at appraisal time.

> Keep a record of what you've achieved so your work isn't forgotten.

> Where it's relevant and appropriate raise your ideas at meetings.

Write about your ideas in a formal letter or report to the line manager. That way it stands the best chance of being passed on up the line.

When you're networking make sure people know about your ideas. If the ideas are good people will talk about them and maybe want to use them.

If you have a staff suggestion scheme use it.

If you have a staff journal and you can work your ideas into it, do so.

Look for opportunities to give talks and presentations on your ideas.

Network, write, and speak outside your organization through professional associations, network groups, and local contacts.

Consider writing a piece for your professional journal, local newspaper, or the national press.

Start a blog and use social media sites.

# CREATING OPPORTUNITIES

> *Developing awareness of opportunities that offer a match with self-identity and long-term career direction, and constantly searching for training and educational development that will help you achieve your potential.*

## WHY DO IT?

Organizational life has changed. It used to be that people in the traditional professions such as accountancy, law, teaching, and so on had careers and most of us had jobs. Now more people feel they want a career and are willing to work towards that goal. But few organizations have the time, or resources, or the political will to set up career management and support services other than for special groups such as graduates and so called high flyers. So most of us are left to our own devices. The people who discover the art of creating opportunities for themselves will be the people who have most success in their careers.

## SELF-AWARENESS

Self-awareness is the first step. Having a sense of career and life direction, and knowing your strengths and development needs, helps you know which opportunities are right for you and where you should start looking for them. From the work you've done on forging the armour of self-awareness learn your personal characteristics of motivation, ability, personality until they become second nature. Then select the opportunities which best match them. Work out what training and education you need to take advantage of the opportunities that appeal to you and go get them. This way you develop in a proper context rather than bouncing from one set of unrelated ideas to another.

## ORGANIZATIONAL POLITICS

Keep your ear to the ground, get to know what's going on in your organization, and find out who are the 'in' people. This is an intelligence gathering exercise to get to know who can be of help to you in creating and developing the opportunities you want.

## NETWORKING

Networking helps you establish contacts in areas of interest to you. Networks don't come to you. You have to go out and find the networks relevant to the field in which you're searching for opportunities, or start one yourself. Get to know organizations and people who have the knowledge, experience, and skills you want. Approach them, talk to them, ask them for help. It's amazing how opportunities pop up unexpectedly once you get involved in networking.

## PROACTIVITY

Search your organization for ideas that need developing, for business opportunities that nobody has yet thought of, for potential problems that nobody has spotted. Do this in areas of your greatest strengths where you're likely to be most successful. Be creative, be innovative, be assertive in chasing your ideas. Spot the chance and go for it.

## PROFESSIONAL QUALIFICATIONS

Two approaches here. First, don't be put off by not having qualifications. If the career role is right for you in terms of match with your personal characteristics of motivation, ability, and personality go for it. If necessary start in a related lower level unqualified position and work up. Lots of people are successful in getting a job where they don't meet the 'essential' professional qualification requirements because they've sold themselves on their obvious motivation, and because they've thought about their past experiences in work, sport, hobbies, and social life and shown how it matches the requirements of the post they want.

The second approach is to work part-time at getting the right professional qualification. Doing this will give you a great deal of inside information about the career role you want, will bring you into contact with people already doing that kind of work, and will help you develop good network contacts. Contact the relevant Institute or Association and ask for career information and details of professional qualifications.

## EDUCATION

As for professional qualifications, don't be put off by lack of them. But do consider developing your education. Education broadens the mind, creates awareness of new possibilities, opens windows of opportunity. And if you choose subjects related to your motivation they'll be exciting and energizing. You'll feel you've embarked on a journey of discovery that will lead you to new horizons. And new horizons are what you will find through education.

Around half of all students in the UK are mature students, and mature means over the age of 21. You can study full-time, part-time, by correspondence tuition, or on the internet. It's sometimes free, sometimes grant aided, but usually it requires money. But don't see it as a cost, see it as an investment in your future. It's not essential to have A levels to get onto a degree course as a mature student. Work experience and access courses are acceptable to most universities.

## JUST DO IT

Creating opportunities is something you can manage for yourself. It takes a little effort and commitment, sometimes a lot. But if you're committed you can exceed your expectations. Most of it is down to attitude. After all, if you don't do it who will do it for you?

# LEADERSHIP

> *Whether leadership of self or leadership of others this is a valuable weapon which often wins the day when other means have failed. It's not necessary to be a formally appointed leader to acquire and use leadership skills.*

## IS IT LEARNED OR INHERITED?

Argument rages, but there are inherent personality characteristics that can help those who have them to develop leadership skills more easily than others. For example, assertiveness, people centredness, warmth and empathy. But history shows us lots of examples of successful leaders who've displayed none of these qualities, so it's hard to take a fixed view. A lot depends on situation and circumstance too, so a good leader in one situation may not perform as well in another.

So can leadership be learned? Yes, if you see leadership as the ability to influence others, of their own free will, to pursue some course of action. The free will bit is important because you can make people pursue a course of action through fear of punishment, or through emotional blackmail, but this is not leadership.

## THE FUNDAMENTALS OF GOOD LEADERSHIP

The definition above carries some implications. For instance all individuals are different, so how successful you are at leading people will depend on your ability to understand their motivation, ability, and personality. A fundamental aspect of leadership, then, is the ability to attend carefully to what individuals say and do, and to learn to analyze the clues people give off about who and what they are.

Remembering that people behave differently in different situations, it is also important to look at the environment in which leadership is required. And then there is the added complication of a task that must be fulfilled by those particular people in that particular environment. It's this mix of people, environment, and task that makes leadership complex. You can't please everybody all of the time, so leadership needs to have a strong element of well established trust to ensure people respond appropriately even when conditions feel wrong for them.

Trust has to be built up over a period of time, and it's done by:

>Understanding individuals and communicating with them in the language of their motivation, ability, and personality.

>Setting a personal example of the values you wish to instil in others.

>Being just and fair in all your relationships.

>Displaying moral courage in the face of adversity.

## GENERAL CHARACTERISTICS OF GOOD LEADERSHIP

The fundamentals of leadership must be learned, practised, and lived. Beyond that there are some basic elements usually associated with good leadership. These are: listening to people and hearing what they say – making people feel valued – recognition – sensible delegation – support – loyalty – setting and maintaining standards – personal example – keeping people informed – feedback – helping people develop themselves – openness.

Here's a simple diagram to show how the elements of good leadership fit together.

*A LEADERSHIP MODEL*

*FUNDAMENTAL QUALITIES OF LEADERSHIP*

- Be just and fair in all you do
- Lead by personal example
- Analyze, understand, and work with people's motivation, ability, and personality
- Develop and show moral courage

*GENERAL CHARACTERISTCS OF GOOD LEADERSHIP*

- Listen and hear
- Make people feel valued
- Give recognition
- Give support
- Show loyalty
- Show openness

- Set and maintain standards
- Delegate sensibly
- Give feedback on performance
- Keep people informed
- Help people develop themselves

# STRESS MANAGEMENT

> *The art of retaining a sense of control over the direction and quality of life. Understanding how to maintain a proper balance between physical and emotional wellbeing.*

## THE BIG WRECKER

Stress can be a major barrier to career and life development because it saps energy, damages self-confidence, and destroys self-esteem. But it's not a disease. You don't catch it, so you don't need to have it.

Essentially stress is about allowing people and situations to take control of your life away from you. So the major recovery element is to regain control. You can learn to manage stress, and you can develop a lifestyle that helps you become stress tolerant.

Stress management is not an optional weapon for Career Warriors. It's essential for coping with the uncertainty and ambiguity encountered in modern organizational life.

## HEALTH WARNING

If you feel stressed, before you start on these stress management ideas go and see your doctor to make sure you have no medical condition that needs treatment. Managing your own stress is not a substitute for proper medical care where medical care is needed.

## HOW YOU CAN BECOME STRESS TOLERANT

Developing a stress tolerant lifestyle requires time and thoughtful effort. It doesn't mean you'll never again be stressed, but it does mean you'll be better able to cope with it when it happens. And you'll be able to recover from it more quickly.

First, it's important to develop a sense of career and life direction because this breeds aspiration, gives hope, and provides the means for a feeling of fulfilment in life. It gives you goals to aim for and a feeling of pride when you achieve them. Successfully managed, life direction will bring self-confidence and self-esteem. Alongside this personal development work it becomes important to follow a lifestyle in which all four clouds shown in the Lifestyle visual (see page 140) are in balance and harmony:

BODY: Work at becoming and staying fit and healthy.

*for the rest of your life*.

MIND: Participate in challenging education and learning.

*for the rest of your life*.

HEART: Don't bottle up your feelings. Acknowledge them, and find someone you trust to talk to about them.

*for the rest of your life.*

SOUL: Practise being a person of honour and integrity. Avoid behaviour that leads to feelings of guilt and shame. Become the kind of person you like and respect. Believe in yourself.

*for the rest of your life*.

AND IN ALL THAT YOU DO APPLY THE THREE BIG Cs

## Control Challenge Commitment

Take control.

See life's ups and downs as challenges rather than problems.

If you're going to do something give it your very best shot.

From these notes I developed three visuals (shown in the following pages) for managers and supervisors so they can pin them to their desks as a constant reminder of how to bring stress management into their daily work routine. I hope you'll find them useful in your work and in your life.

# STRESS SPOTTING

**WHAT IS IT?**

Stress occurs when we believe we aren't able to cope with the problems we face. Often panic can set in and we lose control. Essentially stress is about allowing control of your life to pass from you to people and events surrounding you. By spotting stress symptoms in ourselves we can take action to regain control. Feeling in control is the antidote to stress.

**DANGERS OF BEING OVER STRESSED**

A reasonable amount of anxiety is positive because it gives us the energy and sense of challenge essential to personal achievement. But going over the top on stress can limit our lives because loss of control leads to inactivity, error, increased risk of accident, illness, and exhaustion. Exposure to high levels of stress over a long period of time could put some people at risk of mental breakdown or life threatening disorders such as heart attack.

**TEAM LEADER RESPONSIBILITY**

It's important to monitor yourself for stress symptoms, but also to be on the look out for signs of stress in your team. Apart from the care of people essential to good leadership employers have a responsibility under Health and Safety at Work law to provide a safe working environment. This applies to both mental and physical health.

**WHAT TO LOOK OUT FOR**

*Physical Symptoms* - prolonged periods of unusual breathlessness, indigestion, heart thumping, headaches, muscle aching, tiredness, trembling, sweating, diarrhoea, constipation, frequent urination, impotence.

*Behaviour changes* - anger, irritability, lethargy, sleeplessness and waking early, loss of appetite, over eating, excessive smoking, excessive drinking, withdrawal into self, loss of confidence, feelings of helplessness, accidents, absenteeism, series of minor sickness.

Be sensible about interpreting these signs and symptoms. If you've had a night out on the tiles you could well feel most of these things the following morning. But if you experience any of these over a longer period of time for no apparent reason stop and question what's happening in your life. With your team be constantly aware of people and how they behave, and see any prolonged behaviour change as an alarm signal.

Should you become concerned about any sign or symptom **GO AND SEE YOUR DOCTOR**. The doctor will establish whether the problem is stress related. If the problem occurs for a team member encourage that person to visit their doctor. Don't attempt to manage other people's stress – that's a job for a health professional.

# STRESS BUSTING

**TAKING CONTROL**

All stress reduction techniques are aimed at helping you bring control of your life back within yourself. You can stay in control by learning and understanding stress signs and symptoms, by identifying the events that stress you and planning ahead to avoid or limit their effect, and by learning stress busting techniques.

**IMMEDIATE ACTIONS WHEN YOU FEEL STRESS TAKING CONTROL**

Acknowledge the feeling and handle it.

Stop what you're doing and relax.

Let the shoulders drop and concentrate on easing tension in the face, neck, head, and back.

Breath deeply and slowly from the stomach.

If you can, move away from the situation and get active for ten minutes: e.g. a brisk walk.

Think yourself back into control.

**MEDIUM TERM ACTIONS FOR STRESS MANAGEMENT**

Allow yourself to feel the way you do and discuss your feelings with someone you trust.

Face up to the problem that's bothering you, seeking help to analyze the issues from people with knowledge and skill in that area.

Avoid blaming others but be assertive in expressing your needs.

Develop the habit of optimism and positive thinking.

**LONG TERM ACTIONS FOR DEVELOPING STRESS TOLERANCE**

Work on your personal development through the:

| | |
|---|---|
| HEART | Don't be afraid of your feelings - learn to care about others and about yourself. |
| MIND | Increase your knowledge and skills – constantly inquire and learn. |
| BODY | Maintain good health through a proper balance of exercise and nutrition. |
| SOUL | Create inner strength by developing your own philosophy of life, by believing in yourself, and by establishing a sense of life direction and purpose. |

# DEVELOPING A STRESS TOLERANT LIFESTYLE

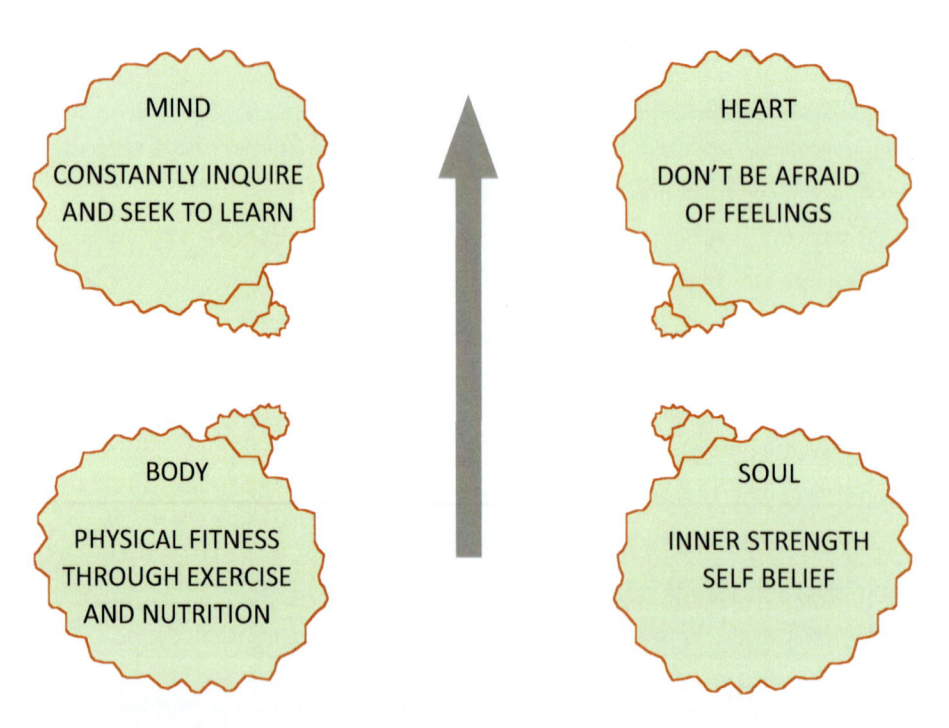

**CAREER AND LIFE DIRECTION**

**MIND**

CONSTANTLY INQUIRE AND SEEK TO LEARN

**HEART**

DON'T BE AFRAID OF FEELINGS

**BODY**

PHYSICAL FITNESS THROUGH EXERCISE AND NUTRITION

**SOUL**

INNER STRENGTH SELF BELIEF

| | |
|---|---|
| CONTROL | Take control of your life |
| CHALLENGE | See things as a challenge rather than a problem |
| COMMITMENT | Give everything in life your best shot |

# ACTION LEARNING

> *A small group of people meeting on a regular basis to improve their self-knowledge and to solve problems preventing them from moving forward in their careers and in their lives.*

Chapter 7 is devoted to Action Learning. It explains how to set up and run an Action Learning set for yourself. Action Learning is the ideal self-help method and, if you can work with a small group of like-minded people, you'll find this a powerful means of career and life development.

# CHECKING THE QUALITY OF MATCH

## YOU – YOUR JOB – THE JOB YOU WANT

## (REFER TO CHAPTER 6)

# CHECKING THE QUALITY OF MATCH

Use this exercise to check the quality of match between yourself and your job. If you aren't in employment use it to check the match with your current life role.

Or maybe you want to look at whether you might find a better match in a different job or life role.

Or why not check out what the match looks like for a more demanding job, or a career role you think might suit you.

Refer back to the MAP exercise you did at page 108 to help you get started.

Don't be afraid to daydream, but do use this exercise as a reality check.

*TO FIND THE ANSWERS TO THE **JOB** SHEETS*
*(see next page)*

*Get a job description.*

*Talk to people who are working in that kind of role.*

*Read the advertising and marketing literature of organizations employing people in career roles that interest you.*

*Go to the library, or if you have one the town careers office, and ask the librarian where you can find books, DVDs, and audio cassettes on the type of work you're interested in.*

*Use the UK Careers Service website (nationalcareersservice.direct.gov.uk) and click on Job Profiles to access extensive information on many careers.*

## WHAT KIND OF MAP DOES IT NEED TO BE SUCCESSFUL IN THE JOB?

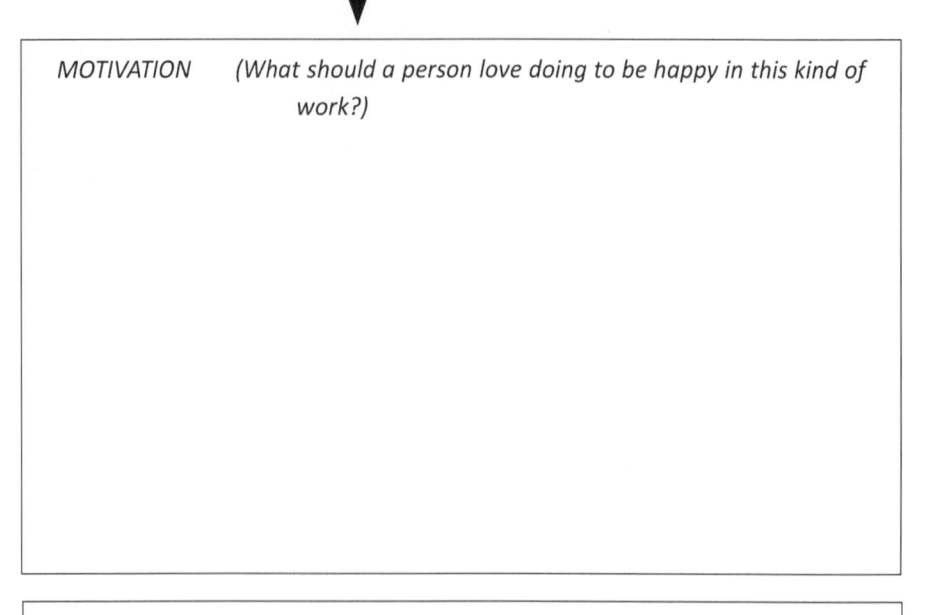

# THE JOB:

---

MOTIVATION  *(What should a person love doing to be happy in this kind of work?)*

---

ABILITY  *(What knowledge, skills, and experience are needed to be successful at this kind of work?)*

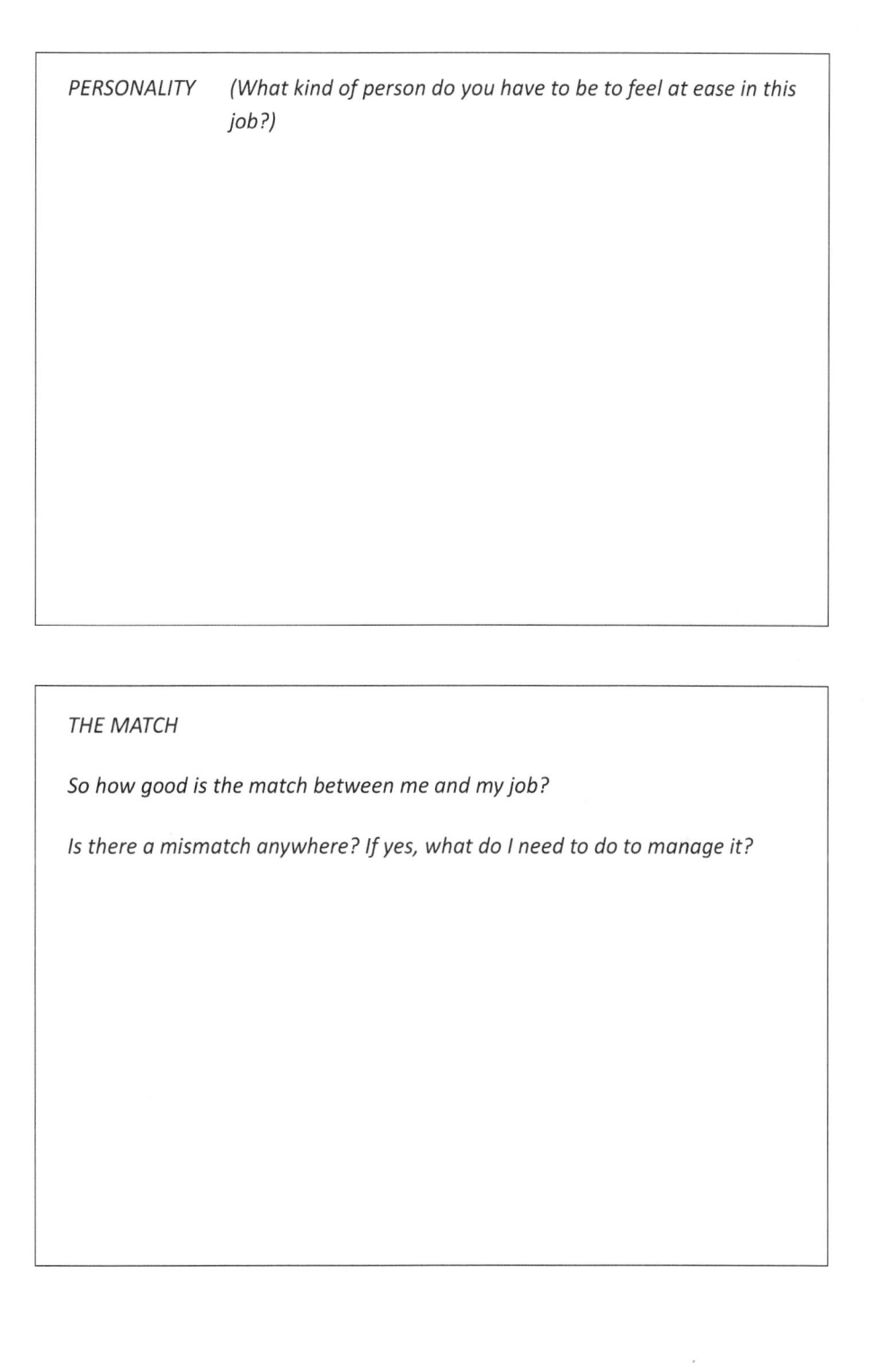

PERSONALITY  (What kind of person do you have to be to feel at ease in this job?)

---

THE MATCH

So how good is the match between me and my job?

Is there a mismatch anywhere? If yes, what do I need to do to manage it?

# SUPER TROUPER

## SPOTLIGHT ON ACTION LEARNING

## (REFER TO CHAPTER 7)

*Super Trouper* is an easy read newsletter designed to help people new to the idea of Action Learning. The idea is to offer some basic understanding to a process which, because it's about learning from experience, can seem at first difficult to understand.

So if you decide to use a similar newsletter keep it simple, and do sprinkle it with colourful photographs, drawings, illustrations, and logos relevant to the people and the organizations involved to make it attractive to them.

The following elements of *Super Trouper* are copyright protected. If you choose to use them you must obtain permission from the following copyright holders:

© The Action Test, The Learning Test, The Real Problem Test. Professor Mike Pedler, Henley Business School, University of Reading, UK.

© The Learning Triangle illustration. Dr Donna Vick, Director, Revans Center Global, USA. (donna.vick@revanscenter.com).

© Photograph of Sycamore Gap, Roman Wall, Northumberland, UK. Andrew Stickland.(andrewstickland@googlemail.com).

# SUPER TROUPER

## Spotlight on Action learning

### Action Learning

Action Learning is about solving complex and difficult problems. But it's also an adult learning environment where colleagues learn through interaction with each other.

This newsletter aims to refresh our minds on the principles and practice of Action Learning. It's useful now and again to step back and reflect on why we do what we do, whether what we do serves a useful purpose, and how we might do it better. Action Learning provides an ideal forum for such issues because it fosters a challenging yet supporting atmosphere for learning.

For those launching into Action Learning for the first time these notes offer a taste of what the process involves. Don't worry if it doesn't make sense. Action Learning is about learning experientially. So it will come with practice.

For the experienced, I hope you'll find this opportunity for reflection useful.

The beauty of Action Learning is its simplicity. Anybody can do it. But if you want to do it effectively and productively you do need some basic guidelines. Everything you need to get started is in this news sheet. The rest? It will happen if the will to make it happen is there.

$$L = P + Q$$

This simple formula represents the essence of Action Learning.

**L** is for learning.

**P** is for programmed knowledge – the kind we get from books, lectures, videos, training courses.

**Q** is for questioning insight.

The point is that it's only by being truly open to the questioning of set colleagues, and reflecting on their questions, that we gain true insight to our problems - and more importantly true insight to our self.

It's the Q that makes Action Learning learning in action.

*Need help with Action Learning?  Tel:  .....................  E:........................@.............*

## Reg Revans - The Father of Action Learning

Whilst Professor Revans was always quick to point out he didn't invent Action Learning, frequently by drawing attention to examples of it in the Old Testament and the teachings of Buddah, there are few who would not attribute its growth to him.

Born in 1907, and active in the Revans Institute for Action Learning and Research at the University of Salford until shortly before his death at the age of 95, Reg's influence spread across the world.

Tributes to his work range from the award of Belgium's Order of Leopold to recognition in Eastern management textbooks of his influence on Japanese management techniques.

A Cambridge research fellow and Olympic athlete (holder of the University of Cambridge undergraduate long jump record for 33 years) it's not hard to see why Reg would have linked learning and activity.

Appointed Assistant for Higher Education for Essex at the age of 28, and later Director of Education for the National Coal Board, it's possible to see the organizational management origins of Action Learning in the 1940s.

Reg reminds us there's nothing new in management, that everything is the reinterpretation of past experience. This is at the heart of Action Learning, and it's this simple idea that accounts for the longevity and success of Action Learning as a management method.

Almost all that's written in this short newsletter draws on the work and writing of this great man.

The core principle is people working together in sets to share their knowledge, skills, and experience in the pursuit of problem solving and personal learning.

The best and most enduring form of learning comes from personal involvement in real problem solving, and from awareness of our thinking and behaviour in that process brought out through disclosure and feedback in a supportive but challenging environment.

That's the kind of development that enables highly effective learning.

## The Place of the Project in Action Learning

The core principle of Action Learning is that people learn best when they engage in purposeful activity which becomes the vehicle for their learning and development.

This is usually a project associated with some aspect of their working life aimed at improving the effectiveness of their role, their department, or their organization.

We work on real issues because simulated problems don't carry the same level of personal involvement in the real world setting. It's the struggle to overcome real world barriers that leads to insightful learning about the world and, more importantly, to knowledge about our self.

This is because knowing is not the same as doing. We can learn the theory of how things are done, but it's the activity of having to tackle problem solving in a real world environment that helps us consolidate our learning in a way we're unlikely to forget.

Action Learning provides the right environment for this kind of learning because the same people meet regularly over a period of time, forming friendships and bonds which encourage an atmosphere of trust.

In this kind of atmosphere we can challenge our behaviour and thinking in a non threatening and supportive way that leads us to new learning, and to the solution of our particular issue.

## So What is Action Learning?

We try to avoid giving tight definitions because the process is so flexible. Once we begin to put boundaries around things it tends to limit their potential. You really have to do Action Learning to understand it properly. But of course people do need to have some idea of what it is they have chosen to participate in. So here are some little golden nuggets of information to illuminate the darkness.

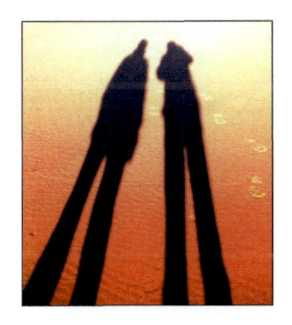

## Action Learning Is

An established and proven method of solving complex and difficult problems through mutual cooperation in a supportive group (called a set in Action Learning).

A way of self managed learning through involvement in real problem solving issues associated with work, career, life.

A set meeting regularly to attack problems of concern to set members.

Regular meetings where thoughts and ideas are discussed and challenged, and where set colleagues support each other in their problem solving activities.

A safe environment where mutual trust and confidentiality exist.

A setting where everybody has equal status and equal opportunity to participate.

A way of learning a lot about yourself.

A safe way of challenging the thinking of others and having one's own thinking challenged without offence being taken or given.

Different from group problem solving methods, or simply learning by doing, because it focuses on challenging inquiry and reflection on personal thinking and behaviour.

## How Set Members Learn From Each Other

These are some of the questions people involved in Action Learning ask themselves about their learning within the set:

Do we all get a fair share of opportunity to speak?

Do we discuss how we are learning from each other?

How do we handle a set member's absence?

Is talk all about task, or are feelings and relationships considered?

Am I less than honest about my feelings during set discussion?

How well do I really listen to the problems and success of others?

Should we make each other accountable for progress?

Do some members seem less committed than others, and can this be discussed in the set?

When I leave a set meeting do I feel better than before I came?

## How Do You Know You're Action Learning?

In an Action Learning set it's easy to lose direction and to end up with a gossip session if we don't apply a bit of discipline to the proceedings.

That's a pity because the power of Action Learning lies in the process of challenging inquiry. So here's a way to test whether we're involved in true Action Learning:

**Action Test:** What evidence is there of ideas being tested in action?

**Learning Test:** What evidence is there of personal development arising from learning within the set?

**Real Problem Test:** What evidence is there of real problems being tackled?

Source: Coghlan, D., and Pedler, M. (2006) Action Learning dissertations: structure, supervision and examination. Action Learning:Research & Practice Vol 3, Issue 2, 127-139.

Ask yourself these questions constantly as your set develops. Discuss and debate them. Apply the answers to your learning.

## Learning From Writing Things Down

A crucial aspect of learning is the monitoring of what it is we've learned. A powerful way of doing this is to record our learning in a journal or learning log. This gives us a permanent record accumulated over time that allows us to revisit our learning experiences, keep track of our development, and avoid forgetting.

Writing things down helps us consolidate our learning because it encourages reflection on what we've learned and its relevance to our work and our lives. It can be a highly creative process generating insight into current problems and issues when we make links between new and old learning.

In Action Learning we build some structure around the process of monitoring our learning, and we make the structure easy to understand by using what we call The Learning Triangle (see below). M is for monitoring which is the core activity. What we monitor, by writing down our learning as it occurs, is:

Work: what we learn from engaging in the problems and issues of our project.

Set: what we learn from participation in our Action Learning set.

Information: what we learn from programmed knowledge such as books, lectures, DVDs, training courses. This is the P of Revans' L = P + Q (see front page).

**In all this learning very often the most significant aspect is what we learn about our self.**

We call this the Botham & Morris Learning Triangle because the model and the ideas behind it were developed by Professor David Botham and Professor John Morris during their time as, respectively, Director and Visiting Professor at the Revans Institute.

The Learning Triangle

Source: Vick, D. (1999). A Study of the Action Learning Process, PhD thesis, University of Salford, England.

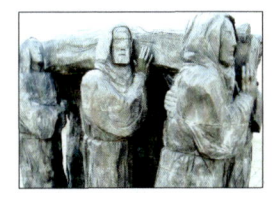

Following the discipline of the Learning Triangle will prove invaluable to anyone intending to write about their project and their learning.

# EXAMPLES OF CAREER OBJECTIVES

## (REFER TO CHAPTER 9)

# EXAMPLES OF CAREER OBJECTIVES

These example objectives will give you some guidance, but only in terms of general structure. Your own objectives will be highly specific to you and put together from your reading and study of this book. How you write your objectives and what you put in them will depend on where you are in your own development, your personal and family circumstances, and your financial situation.

When you've written your objectives test them against the SMART rule repeated here and explained in Chapter 9.

Remember to review and update your objectives frequently.

*SMART OBJECTIVES*

| | |
|---|---|
| *Specific:* | *Objectives should be clear about what exactly is to be achieved (e.g. NVQ Level 3 in Health and Social Care).* |
| *Measurable:* | *Objectives should have a clear outcome that can be assessed against some standard (e.g. attainment of NVQ Level 3).* |
| *Achievable:* | *What you are aiming for should be a realistic goal in line with your previous qualifications and experience and within your resources of time and money.* |
| *Relevant:* | *Your objectives should be linked to where it is you want to be in your career or your life.* |
| *Timed:* | *Your objectives should include a deadline for achieving your goal.* |

# EXAMPLE 1

Colin, a newly appointed first line supervisor in a large insurance company, is beginning to think seriously about his career for the first time.

*SHORT-TERM OBJECTIVES*

1. Clarify my motivation, ability, and personality by working through the MAP Exercise (page 108) by 15 August.

2. Check how I fit with my present career role by working through the Checking The Quality Of Match pages (page 142) by 22 August.

3. Work through my job description noting matches and mismatches between me and my work responsibilities by 29 August.

*LONG-TERM OBJECTIVES*

1. In time for my next appraisal on 1 April next year prepare a learning log showing at least five examples of how I've used my strengths to solve problems at work, and at least three examples of how I've improved my work quality by identifying and working on my personal development.

2. Work towards promotion by taking a part-time course in NVQ Level 3 Business Management Skills. I will sign up for this course with Riverside College at their registration day next August and begin the course in September of next year.

3. At my appraisal on 1 April next year negotiate with my line manager for half-day release and financial support from the company for my Business Management Skills course.

# EXAMPLE 2

Sushila is an English graduate working as a personnel officer. After career guidance she's decided that what she really wants to do is to work as a solicitor specializing in children's law. Sushila lives with her parents who have agreed to support her financially whilst she studies to become qualified.

### SHORT-TERM OBJECTIVES

1. By 15 August contact a local law firm and ask for a networking visit to find out what the ups and downs of life as a children's law solicitor are.

2. By 22 August search the National Careers Service website, or visit the local library reference section, and read up on careers and qualifications in law.

3. By 29 August contact The Law Society and ask for advice on which universities and colleges in this region offer Common Professional Examination (CPE) courses and check that this will qualify me for entry to Law School.

### MEDIUM-TERM OBJECTIVES

1. By 31 January next year complete an application for a place on a CPE course commencing the following autumn.

2. On completion of the CPE course start one year solicitor final examination course.

### LONG-TERM OBJECTIVE

1. Four years from now be working in a law firm as a trainee in child law.

# EXAMPLE 3

Zak had a troubled time at school and left with no qualifications, but he's done well in his local authority as an administrative officer. Some of his in-house training courses have given him the skills to train new entrants and this put the idea in his mind that he'd like to become a teacher. After visiting his old school and talking to a couple of teachers he liked and respected, Zak decides to go for it. He's married with two children so cannot afford to quit his job. He doesn't want to put all his eggs in one basket at this stage but does want to work towards a degree qualification so decides to study with the Open University in subjects relevant to his present job before making a final commitment to teaching.

### SHORT-TERM OBJECTIVES

1. Discuss career change implications for family with my wife by 15 August.

2. By 22 August contact personnel department to check on career development support opportunities.

3. Also by 22 August contact National Careers Service to get information on financial support options.

4. By 29 August have searched Open University website for degree courses that interest me. Alternatively contact my Open University regional office and ask for information on degree courses.

### LONG-TERM OBJECTIVES

1. Complete OU degree by............

2. Complete OU Post Graduate Certificate in Education course by the end of............

3. Find a teaching position and start work by..............

# A FRAMEWORK FOR ORGANIZATIONAL GOOD PRACTICE IN CAREER SELF-MANAGEMENT

(REFER TO CHAPTER 3)

# A FRAMEWORK FOR ORGANIZATIONAL GOOD PRACTICE IN CAREER SELF-MANAGEMENT

## BUILDING THE STRUCTURE

Behind good practice in career self-management lies an awareness of the need to understand people as individuals, and to help them take responsibility for the process of seeking personal satisfaction in their work. In short, organizations need to help people help themselves to become self-developers. Forward looking organizations are already doing this, but there aren't many of them.

There are a number of actions that organizations should take to promote the idea of career self-management:

### *Develop And Propagate A Strategy*

Isolated initiatives are useless because they are not driven by a broader organizational requirement, so they quickly wither and die. A strategy statement should be so framed that every initiative related to it can be justified in terms of the strategy. What cannot be justified is not included. Publish and communicate the strategy, and from the top level of the organization believe it and live it.

### *Involve Trade Unions*

Where trade unions form part of the organizational structure representatives should be involved in career development strategy formation from the outset. There is often a deep distrust of management motives, particularly where career management and counselling are involved because they can be seen as preparation for the next round of redundancy. Not only can union involvement help bridge this credibility gap, union officials are usually well placed, and often highly trained, to act as learning facilitators.

## Provide An Appropriate Organizational Culture

If the prevailing organizational culture does not encourage and support self-development it will not work. Staff will expect managers to lead by example and to become role models for their own behaviour. Two fundamental elements of success will be the public attitude of every manager from the chief executive right through the organization, and a performance appraisal system that includes requiring managers to demonstrate commitment to developing their staff.

## Set Up A Development Centre

A development centre can be grand or simple, but it must be highly visible because it provides a tangible demonstration of the organization's commitment to supporting people. It's a place people can visit to find out who they can talk to about their career thinking (usually in confidence), where they can get advice about their career ideas, and where they can access career and personal development literature.

## Provide Professional Career Guidance

Whether staff are trained in house to provide this service, or whether the service is obtained from external sources, expert analysis and guidance from trained professionals is crucial to helping people establish a good sense of career identity and direction.

## Introduce An Awareness Programme

This is usually done through a series of self-development workshops at which the company strategy is explained and people are made aware of what resources are available to help them. It can be difficult to come to terms with the idea of having to manage your own career, and with a concept of career development which does not necessarily include promotion, so people need help in refocusing their approach.

## Develop Managers' Skills

Managers need to develop coaching and elementary counselling skills, the most important of which are listening and motivating, so they are in a position to provide help and support to their staff. It's not normally the line manager's function to develop professional counselling skills, so trained support should be available either from personnel staff or through external providers.

### Introduce Individual Career Tracking Systems

There are several ways of doing this, whether paper based or electronically. The most basic requirement is an Individual Development Plan, owned and completed by individuals, which is used as a written record of how both short-term work related development and longer-term personal development will take place. This is negotiated between individual and manager at least once a year and ideally quarterly. People should be provided with a system within which they can record their goals and achievements, their appraisals and development plans. They should be encouraged in the art of keeping a learning log or learning journal.

### Advertise Internal Vacancies

Offering employees opportunities to move within the organization encourages staff retention and helps people widen their horizons. The system must be fair, and behind the scenes dealing for jobs must be eliminated.

## MOVE FORWARD WITH CAUTION

These practical steps are simply organizational tools, and just as all individuals are different so too are all organizations. It would be wrong, therefore, to lift any successful programme from one organization and transfer it to another. Picking up the theories and practices is fine, but they must be repackaged in the light of a particular organization's culture and objectives. The need for an integrated strategy that includes management of the cultural aspects of the organization is the vital thread that has to be woven right through every facet of a career self-management programme.

Be aware that the path of career self-management will not be without problems since it encourages individuals to become engaged in personal lifetime development that transcends the present. The job or the organization may not provide the right environment for their personal growth, so they may have to make a change.

Even if the job is right and the organization appropriate, self-developers are likely to grow to question the way things are done, to challenge the established order of things, and to come up with new ideas. Sometimes this upsets people in authority because they feel threatened by it, so for self-development to flourish the organizational culture needs to be one that welcomes challenge and new ideas. Launched without this understanding, the creative thinking and innovative ideas that hallmark career self-management will wither and die.

Finally, not everyone will see their life development in terms of career and no amount of persuasion or coercion will change that view. This should not be seen as a failure on the part of the individual or the organization, nor is it! That's life, and it needs to be managed in some other way.

# NOTES TO CHAPTERS

Much of what I've learned about career self-management is experience driven but, as I pointed out at the end of Chapter 1, I've also absorbed a great deal of learning through education and research and the many knowledgeable people I've been able to associate with. Sometimes it's difficult to recall which came first.

These notes are clearly not an exhaustive list of what I've read and who I've listened to. People significant in my learning and development are included in the Acknowledgements section. The following notes refer to the major sources from which I recall having drawn insight and inspiration, and which I've found useful during the development of my thinking and ideas.

I accept that in my study of career theory and practice I will have absorbed ideas from many other sources long forgotten. I therefore apologize to anyone who feels I've overlooked their contribution.

## Chapter 1

1. The Why do it for yourself? section of this chapter and Why career self-management has become an issue section of Chapter 3 are closely linked. In writing these sections I've leaned on the evidence of several research reports and observer comments including these:

    Chartered Institute of Personnel and Development executive briefing The Future of Careers. (2002). London: CIPD.

Chartered Institute of Personnel and Development research report Understanding the People and Performance Link. (2003). London: CIPD.

Chartered Institute of Personnel and Development research report Creating An Engaged Workforce. (2010). London: CIPD.

Confederation of British Industry Report of the Vocational Education and Training Task Force: Towards a skills revolution. (1989).

Jackson, C., Arnold, J., Nicholson, N. & Watts, A. G. (1996). Managing careers in 2000 and beyond. University of Sussex: Institute for Employment Studies Report 304.

Monks, J. (1996). in Partners for Lifelong Learning. Trades Union Congress pamphlet. London: Congress House.

Patterson, M., West, M., Lawthorn, R. & Nickell, S. (1997). Impact of people management practices on business performance. Chartered Institute of Personnel and Development Issues in People Management No 22. London: CIPD.

2. Mental imagery. Taken from my PhD research Stickland, R. (2001). Dawn of the Career Warrior, Chapter 10. University of Salford. Influenced initially by general reading on visioning success in sport and later from reading neuroscience literature.

Waring, P. (2008). Coaching the brain. The Coaching Psychologist, Vol 4, No 2, August 2008, 63-70.

The Royal Society Policy Document 02/11. (2011). Brain Waves Module 2: Neuroscience: implications for education and lifelong learning. (ISBN 978-0-85403-880-0).

3. Action Learning. See notes to Chapter 7, Note 8.

## Chapter 2

4. Career Warrior weapons. Reflecting on this list now it seems obvious that what I gleaned from experience must be informed by other forms of learning. Much of what I absorbed came from a number of management courses completed during my career in the Royal Air Force, perhaps from 1969 onward.

   Interpersonal Skills was probably the first area in which I began to read about the theoretical perspectives behind practices that seemed obvious to me as a manager, and this I would attribute largely to Ed Schein writing about employee motivation in Schein, E. (1965). Organizational psychology. Englewood Cliffs, NJ: Prentice-Hall.

   Action Learning See notes to Chapter 7, Note 8.

   Stress management had not originally occurred to me as a topic related to career development until I began, in 1994, to run training courses and seminars on it whilst working as an internal career consultant with a financial services company. During that period I joined a seminar at Cambridge University run by Dr Pietro Pizzo, an Italian clinical oncologist and psychotherapist who is helping people take responsibility for their own health as part of a holistic approach to cancer prevention and cure. Two things struck me about the doctor's teaching: the idea of a relationship between negative feelings about work and susceptibility to illness, and the thought that individuals are able to take responsibility for the successful management of their own health. This closely parallels my thinking on career satisfaction and sense of wellbeing, and a conviction that the solution lies in one's own hands through career self-management.

   Creating opportunities was a latecomer to the list, introduced after discovering the DOTS model of careers guidance based on experience in schools in Law, B. & Watts, A. (1977). Schools, careers, and community. London: Church Information Office.

Leadership is something I lived and breathed during a career in the armed forces. My skill and knowledge development came from military training, through learning based on observation of the good and bad example of others, and from the successful and unsuccessful outcomes of my own leadership style. And whilst I have read and perhaps been influenced by countless books and articles my experience of them is that they have taught me little new. They confirm what I've learned from life. And so the leadership element of Career Warrior reflects my own experiential learning.

The remaining weapons of self-marketing, networking, organizational politics, and proactivity are not gleaned from literature. They come from the conviction, based on experience of helping people to help themselves, that they are crucial to the process of career self-management.

## Chapter 3

5. Why career self-management has become an issue. See notes to Chapter 1, Note 1.

## Chapter 4

6. Motivation, aptitude, personality. I first came across this structure as a trainee psychologist under the tutelage of Joshua Fox, my psychology director at the London career consultancy where I began my second career. Later, when researching for my PhD, I found a more formal exposition at Miller, M. (1991). The integration of psychometric test results within guidance counselling. Guidance and Assessment Review, 7(2), 5-7.

## Chapter 6

7. Matching self and job. From a practical point of view the idea of matching self-identity to career role seemed obvious, as it did to others long before me. I first read about person/job matching in Holland, J. (1973). Making vocational choices: a theory of careers. Englewood Cliffs, NJ: Prentice-Hall. Later I found an earlier approach, perhaps the first in career theory, in Parsons, F. (1909). Choosing a vocation. Boston: Houghton Mifflin.

## Chapter 7

8. Action Learning. Drawn from lengthy experience of being an Action Learning set member as part requirement of my PhD programme at the University of Salford Revans Institute for Action Learning and Research, and from several years of practice setting up and facilitating Action Learning programmes. At the Revans Institute I gained considerable insight into the philosophy and practice of Action Learning from close involvement with Institute staff. (See acknowledgements for details of individuals).

   I count myself particularly fortunate to have met and spent a little time with Professor Reg Revans. I learned about Action Learning and I learned about myself from those meetings. My Action Learning work is firmly rooted in Revans, R. (1983). The ABC of Action Learning. Bromley: Chartwell-Bratt (now out of print but see 2011 edition published by Gower).

## Chapter 8

9. The Learning Triangle. The philosophy of the Learning Triangle was developed by Professors David Botham (Director) and John Morris (Visiting Professor) during their time at the Revans

Institute for Action Learning and Research at the University of Salford circa 1995/1996. As new postgraduate research students at the Institute in 1996 we were introduced to the Learning Triangle as both a means of monitoring our learning during Action Learning set meetings and as a tool for thesis writing, so I had five years of exposure to it.

One of my Action Learning set colleagues, Revans Scholar Donna Vick, now Dr Vick, explored the philosophy as part of her PhD thesis and produced the illustration I use in Chapter 8 and as part of the *Super Trouper* newsletter, reproduced in the Treasure Chest section in Part 4. Donna kindly gave me permission to reproduce her illustration cited in Vick, D. (1999). A Study of the Action Learning Process. PhD thesis, University of Salford, England.

## The Treasure Chest

10. In the newsletter *Super Trouper*, which I give to all my new Action Learning set participants, and to anyone expressing an interest in knowing more about Action Learning, I include a section titled How Do You Know You're Action Learning? I'm indebted to Professor Mike Pedler for this set of rules which is a direct extract from his work developed at the Revans Institute for Action Learning and Research (in Coghlan, D and Pedler, M. (2006). Action Learning dissertations: structure, supervision and examination, Action Learning: Research & Practice Vol 3, Issue 2, 127-139, Autumn 2006).

# INDEX

Action Learning 9, 19
    how to do it 61-79
    newsletter *Super Trouper* 63, 146-151
    power of questions 63, 65
    Reg Revans 62
    why it fails 77-79
aptitude 15, 39, 41, 109
armour, weapons, and wiles 7-8, 15-21, 35
assertiveness 117, 132
avatar 7

Campbell, Sir Malcolm, 24
career
    as a quest 7, 8, 12, 13-14
    as a story 7, 80-81
    confusion 15, 17, 25, 36, 53
    language 4, 7, 15, 41, 44, 53, 77, 124, 133
    long-term 6, 19, 25-26
    objectives 87-93, 152-156
    transitions 6
    uncertainty 17, 19, 20, 49, 50, 53, 135
career coach 16, 41
    checking quality of 106-107
career navigation 20, 21
    process 49-57
    towards dream job 56
career self-management 24-31
    case for 28-31
    good practice in organizations 30-31, 157-161
    impact on you 25-27
    impact on organization 27-28
    why do it? 4-6
career guidance
    national websites 104
    free help 41, 104
    professional help 41-42, 103-107
    psychometric testing 41, 43, 107
    without professional help 42-43
Career Warrior
    armour 7, 8, 15-16, 21, 35-44
    overview 7-8, 13-23
    weapons 7, 8, 17-19, 45-47, 113-141
    what Career Warriors say 95-99
    wiles 7, 8, 20, 48
change and chaos 23
creating opportunities 19, 126, 129-131

experiential learning 17, 147

fulfilment 3, 9, 15, 52, 82, 87, 93, 136

goals 14, 20, 49, 88-90, 136

happiness 3
hero 13, 21-22

internet 43, 67, 125, 131
interpersonal skills 18, 123-124, 127

job satisfaction 3, 15, 26, 52, 82, 87, 93, 109

lateral thinking 48
leadership 19, 46, 127, 132-134
    model of 134
learning log/journal 80-86, 151
    added value of 85-86
    example of 83
Learning Triangle 84-85, 151
life mission statement 92-93

MAP 15-16
    triangle 38-40
    exercise 42, 44, 108-112

matching self and job 21
    process and pictures 51-56
    mismatch 21, 35, 49-50, 52-56
    quality of match exercise 56, 142-145
mental imagery 7-8, 13-14, 21, 35, 38
motivation, ability, personality 4, 15-16, 19, 21, 38-42, 53, 93, 108-112
National Careers Services in UK 57, 104, 143
networking 18, 57, 118-119, 127, 130
notes to chapters 12, 162-167

objective setting 87-94
    examples 92, 152-156
    general rules for setting 90, 153
    ideals and reality 88-89
organizational fog 20, 50
organizational politics 18, 120-122, 127, 130

proactivity 18, 126-128, 130
psychometric testing 41, 43, 107

quality of match exercise 142-145

Revans, Reg 62, 148

search for the hero 13, 21-22
self-awareness 15, 36, 49, 82
    a structure for 37-39
self
    confidence 46, 49, 83, 88, 117, 135, 136
    esteem 36, 49, 117, 135, 136
    help books 43
    identity 21, 37-38, 48, 49, 50, 53, 92, 122
    marketing 17, 115-117

short termism 5, 6
shrinking workforce 5, 6
SMART objectives 90, 153
snowstorm effect 36, 53

stress
    busting 139
    developing stress tolerant lifestyle 87, 135-136, 140
    management 19, 87, 135-140
    spotting 138
*Super Trouper* 63, 70, 146-151

treasure chest 11, 101-102
true potential 4, 15, 16, 22, 31, 44, 82, 89, 92

waymarkers 87, 88, 89
weapons 7, 8, 17-19, 45-47, 49, 113-141
wiles 7, 8, 20-21, 48